Aarron Walter

D0970866

DESIGNING
FOR EMOTION

Publisher: Jeffrey Zeldman
Designer: Jason Santa Maria
Managing Editor: Mandy Brown
Editor: Krista Stevens
Copyeditor: Rose Weisburd
Compositor: Rob Weychert

ISBN 978-1-937557-00-3

A Book Apart
New York, New York
http://abookapart.com

10 9 8 7 6 5 4 3 2 1

TABLE OF CONTENTS

For Jamie & Olivier, who inspire the most meaningful emotional experiences in my life.

FOREWORD

We want our work to stand out from the rest. We want people to have such a great experience that they feel the need to talk about it to everyone. We want what we make to be remarkable.

Often those seeking remarkability get it for just a moment. Some have achieved their goal of joyful office watercooler discussions by creating a thiry-second Superbowl Spot with something as simple a handful of slothful individuals answering their phone with an exaggerated "WHAAATS AAAWWP?" Others get it with a viral video of dogs on skateboards. But these are just quick flashes in the pan.

The real payoff comes when we can make that remarkability last. When we can make people continually feel our work is worthy of discussion. When—for weeks, months, maybe even years—the people who engage with our work continue to sing its praises to everybody they meet.

Long-term remarkability translates into the holy grail of the advertising world: word of mouth. When we reach this pinacle of mind-share success, we see our popularity grow, along with the revenues from whichever business model backs it.

But remarkability only happens when we've achieved another plateau: *delight*. People only voluntarily recommend that which is truly delightful. If we want to achieve long-term remarkability, we need to build in long-term delight.

In the pages that follow, Aarron does a (dare I say?) remarkable job of getting us started on creating designs that bring with them an emotional attachment. And with his help, we can sustain the joy to get the long-term effects we're seeking.

Heed Aarron's words carefully. He's put a lot of research and theory into an easily accessible package. A package that will get you started on your own journey to creating designs that inspire a positive emotional response in your users. That journey will take you beyond remarkable.

—Jared Spool
CEO and Founding Principal, User Interface Engineering

1

EMOTIONAL DESIGN

REVOLUTION: SOMETHING LOST AND SOMETHING FOUND

POWERED BY A CHAIN REACTION of ideas and innovations, a revolution of industry swept the western hemisphere in the late eighteenth and nineteenth centuries. In a relatively short time, we discovered ways to transform mined materials into manufacturing devices, transportation systems, and agricultural tools that fueled the twentieth century's explosive innovations. Inventions like the cotton gin, machine tools, the steam engine, the telegraph, and the telephone promised a future filled with opportunity and prosperity.

Though the industrial revolution sprang from a utopian vision of human progress, humans were so often the ones left behind. Skilled craftsmen like blacksmiths, cobblers, tinsmiths, weavers, and many others slowly forfeited their trade to factories that could produce goods faster and at a lower cost. As the machine found its place in our world, the human hand's presence in everyday objects slowly faded.

But some challenged the blind march toward progress. As mass production expanded in the mid-nineteenth century, the Arts and Crafts movement sought to preserve the craftsman's role in domestic goods production, and with it the human touch. The founders of the Arts and Crafts movement revered the things they designed, built, and used every day. They recognized that a craftsman leaves a bit of themselves in their work, a true gift that can be enjoyed for many years.

In the present day, we can see a few parallels. In a quest for higher crop yields and lower production costs, farms have become headless corporations pitting profits against human welfare. But local farmers are finding new markets as consumers search for food produced by people for people. While big-box stores proliferate disposable mass-market goods, websites like Etsy and Kickstarter are empowering artists, craftspeople, and DIY inventors who sell goods they've designed and created. And their customers love the experience. When you buy from an independent craftsman, you support creative thinking and families (not corporations), and you gain the opportunity to live with an object that has a story. That feels good.

We web designers find ourselves in a similar situation. There's plenty of opportunity to build fast and cheap sites with no reverence for craft or the relationship we build with our audience. We could create new projects with stock photography, boilerplate templates, and one-size-fits-all copy. We could reduce our industry to a commodities race, like those who manufactured the industrial revolution. There is a market for that kind of work.

Or we could follow a different path, one paved by the artists, designers, and architects of the Arts and Crafts movement, who believed that preserving the human touch and showing ourselves in our work isn't optional. It's *essential*.

I'm delighted to report that many on the web are already on this path. I'll guide you through examples of the principles that emotional design visionaries use not only to build a human connection with their audience, but also to fuel their success. There's a common thread through these principles—emotional design—which uses psychology and craftsmanship to create an experience for users that makes them feel like there's a person, not a machine, at the other end of the connection.

It's taken our medium time to mature to where we can begin exploring emotional design and talking to our audience with a new voice. Once upon a time, on a web not so unlike the one we enjoy today, we spoke much differently because we hadn't yet learned to be ourselves. We were still trying to be the machine.

THE WAY WE WERE

The web had a rocky start in building emotional connections. It gets gold stars for connecting people in far-off lands, but the necessities of academia were the mother of its inventions— a dry origin indeed. As business pioneers discovered new watering holes, the web quickly became a breeding ground of dot-com bubble thinking. I remember writing copy for my personal website in the late 1990s using the royal "we," trying to create the perception that I was a big company when the guy behind those words was in his bedroom in smelly pajamas trying to figure out HTML. I wasn't trying to be me—I was trying to be like the other big players out there.

But something happened to that trend in the middle of the naughts. All of those people who were laid off or fired after the dot-com bubble burst either started new companies or retreated to their bedrooms and stayed in pajamas to make new websites and applications.

Maybe it was because a boss wasn't standing over their shoulder, or maybe they needed to do something to lift their spirits, but the voice of these new sites was decidedly more personal.

During this period, Flickr launched with the famously familiar and endearing copy that puts smiles on so many faces. Facebook and Twitter surfaced and influenced the voice of the web. These new social tools allowed users to share the minutiae of daily life. That may not sound terribly profound, but it represents a major change in the way that we communicate on the web. Whereas professionalism might have buttoned down our communiqués before social networks, today

FIG 1.1: Dear Rainn Wilson, TMI.

conversations are often more true to the way that we'd speak to friends. Of course, a little moderation is sometimes in order (I'm looking at you, Rainn Wilson, http://bkaprt.com/de/1; FIG 1.1).

The curtain has been drawn back, exposing our humor, grumpiness, concern, stress, and all the other emotions that season our days. As we'll see in Chapter 3, this honesty is creeping into the personalities we craft for our businesses, and our users are beginning to expect the websites and web applications they visit to reflect a personality that they can relate to.

This book is chock-full of examples of a design sensibility that is distinctly human, individual, reflective of a real personality, and honest—all while keeping business goals in mind. You might have some trepidation about how to implement emotional design techniques without boiling your boss's blood. We'll see practical, real-world examples designed to inspire and support your case for employing emotional design in your next project. I'll even share a bevy of data to help you make an empirical case for emotional design.

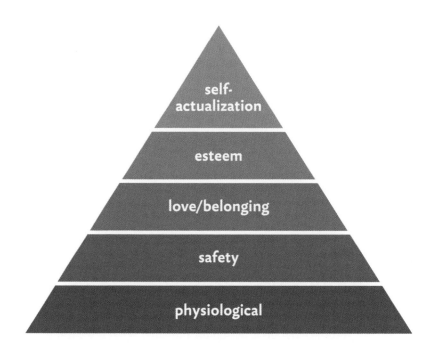

FIG 1.2: Maslow's Hierarchy of Needs.

Keep in mind that ignoring human needs is not a history we are doomed to repeat. Through our designs, we can see and connect with other human beings.

So where do we start? Well, like any good user experience designer, we begin by understanding the needs of the people we're designing for.

HELLO, MASLOW

In the 1950s and 60s, the American psychologist Abraham Maslow discovered something that we all knew but had yet to put into words: no matter our age, gender, race, or station in life, we all have basic needs that must be met. Maslow illustrated his ideas in a pyramid he called the Hierarchy of Needs (FIG 1.2).

Maslow stressed that the physiological needs at the base of this hierarchy must be met first. The need to breathe, eat, sleep, and answer the call of nature trump all other needs in our life. From there, we need a sense of safety. We can't be happy if we fear bodily harm, loss of family, property, or a job. Next, we need a sense of belonging. We need to feel loved and intimately connected to other humans. This helps us get to the next level: a sense of self, a respect for others, and the confidence we need to excel in life. At the top of Maslow's pyramid is a broad, but important category—self-actualization. Once all other needs are met, we can fulfill our need to be creative, to solve problems, and to follow a moral code to serve others.

Maslow's approach to identifying human needs can help us understand our goals when designing interfaces. We could certainly live contented lives meeting only the bottom three strata of the needs pyramid—physiological comfort, safety, and belonging. But it's in that top layer that we can live a truly fulfilled life.

Interface design is design for humans. What if we translated Maslow's model of human needs into the needs of our users? It might look something like this (**FIG 1.3**):

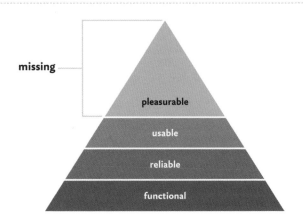

FIG 1.3: We can remap Maslow's Hierarchy of Needs to the needs of our users.

GETTING THE BASICS RIGHT

For a user's needs to be met, *an interface must be functional.*
If the user can't complete a task, they certainly won't spend
much time with an application. Remember when Apple released Ping? It was their attempt at building a social network
around your iTunes music library. It was a pretty big flop, in
part because you couldn't share a song with friends on Twitter
or Facebook. After users learned that the new system lacked
basic features, most didn't return.

The interface must be reliable. There was a stretch of time
when early Twitter adopters learned to hate the "fail whale,"
shown when the server was down or over capacity. If the web
server drops out intermittently, or the service is otherwise
unreliable, a user will leave.

An interface must be usable. It should be relatively easy to
learn to perform basic tasks quickly, without a lot of relearning. Ever tried to book a flight online? If you have, I'd bet a
five spot that expletives tripped across your tongue while each
page loaded. You're not alone. Fortunately, Hipmunk (http://
hipmunk.com) is setting a new bar for online travel booking.

Historically, usability has been the zenith of interface
design. Isn't that a bit depressing? If you can make a usable
interface, you're doing well in our industry. Imagine if we
used that stick to measure success in the auto industry. By that
standard, we'd be swooning over the 1978 AMC Pacer.

Many websites and applications are creating an even better
experience. They're redrawing the hierarchy of needs to include a new top tier with pleasure, fun, joy, and delight. What
if an interface could help you complete a critical task and put
a smile on your face? Well, that would be powerful indeed!
That would be an experience you'd recommend to a friend;
that would be an idea worth spreading.

We need a new yardstick to measure the success of our designs. We can transcend usability to create truly extraordinary
experiences.

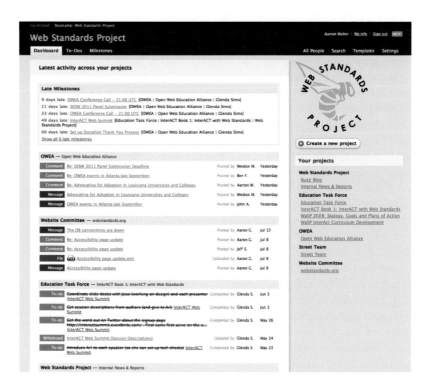

FIG 1.4: Basecamp, a project management web application.

USABLE = EDIBLE

If you're working on the web, chances are you've used 37Signals' handy project management app Basecamp (http://basecamphq.com) (**FIG 1.4**).

In building Basecamp, 37Signals' design ethos centered around simplicity and usability. Their design ideas, summed up in *Getting Real* (http://bkaprt.com/de/2) inspired a generation of web pros to keep designs simple and make sure tasks are easy to complete.

37Signals helped us tackle the bottom of the needs pyramid. With a zeal for simplicity and spartan design, they create eminently functional, reliable, and usable web apps. Despite user requests for new features or changes to the workflow, Basecamp has remained true to its original vision. That's both a strength and a weakness. With few major changes over the years, the interface is predictable, usable, and requires almost no relearning. But an interface that doesn't evolve risks losing touch with user needs. The same is true of design thinking. Though the 37Signals design ethos guided us in the infancy of our medium, the landscape of the web and our relationship to it has changed. Simple and usable is great, but there's still more we can achieve. We must bring web design back into the realm of delight.

Think back to the best meal you've ever had. Not a good meal, I mean a mind-blowing, palate-challenging, fall-in-love-with-food-again, great meal. What made it so memorable? Was it the taste and texture of the food? Was it the unexpected pairing of flavors? Was it the artful presentation, attentive wait staff, and ambiance? Chances are, many of these factors worked in concert to elicit an intense emotional response.

Now think about this. Did you once think about the meal's nutritional value? I doubt it (if you did, you need to get out a little more). Though the meal met your body's needs, the immense pleasure of the experience formed the memory in your brain, one which you will carry for a long time.

Why don't we aim for a similar target in web design? We've been designing usable interfaces, which is like a chef cooking edible food. Certainly we all want to eat edible foods with nutritional value, but we also crave flavor. Why do we settle for usable when we can make interfaces both usable and pleasurable?

Well, Wufoo isn't settling. They're making their usable interface fun.

Wufoo: more than usable

Wufoo (http://wufoo.com/), a popular web app that helps people build forms and connect them to databases, has emotional design baked right into the interface (**FIG 1.5**). Like Basecamp, Wufoo serves a utilitarian purpose. Its users want to perform tasks quickly. Making databases and designing forms can be

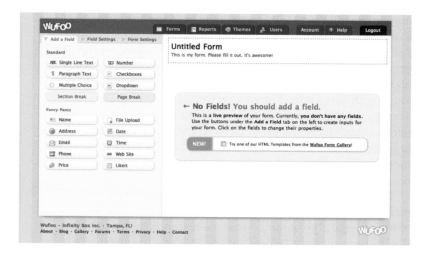

FIG 1.5: Wufoo, a form building web app that is more than usable, it's fun!

tricky and intimidating if you're not very technical. But Wufoo makes it easy and, unlike most of its competitors, they make it fun.

Wufoo keeps task flows simple and focused with uncluttered interfaces. Though the app offers powerful features, it strikes a healthy balance by not including obscure functionality that might confuse the majority of users while serving a niche audience. With millions of users creating bajillions of forms, it's fair to say that Wufoo is reliable. Like Basecamp, it's doing a heck of a job staying functional, reliable, and usable for a big audience.

But there's one big, big difference with Wufoo's user experience: personality. Spend a couple of minutes in the app, and you'll get a sense for the people who made the application. It shines through in the copy. "O, what men dare do!" greets me at the top of the Form Builder dashboard, a hat tip to William Shakespeare. And again, in the sample copy atop a fresh form awaiting customization, "This is my form. Please fill it out. It's awesome!" Note the primary colors on each page; sans-serif typefaces chat in familiar, informal tones. There aren't many hard edges here. Corner radii are generous, creating a cartoony feel. Even if you've never met the guys who made this app, you know what makes them tick when you log into your account. Their voice and perspective comes through in their designs. Wufoo is a piece of software, but it feels like a living, breathing human being.

Kevin Hale, the user experience design lead and co-founder of Wufoo, considered the emotional state of Wufoo users when conceptualizing the design.

> *The inspiration for our color palette came from our competitors. It was really depressing to see so much software designed to remind people they're making databases in a windowless office, and so we immediately knew we wanted to go in the opposite direction.*

In his mind, Kevin had an emotional portrait of the people he was designing for. They're "people in a windowless office," probably under the thumb of a boss who needs them to collect information. They're on deadline and uninspired by their day-to-day work. With a clear personality in the application that says it's okay to have a little fun at work, he's delivering warmth to thousands of cold, gray cubicles. That's something people won't forget, and for good reason.

There's craftsmanship in Wufoo, but I'm not referring just to the technical construction. A craftsman wields great technical skill, and shows us their hand in their work. Their work exudes a human quality we can see and feel. We could list the design elements that work in concert in Wufoo to construct a personality that users can relate to, but the sum is greater than its parts. As we'll see in Chapter 4, Wufoo uses emotional engagement to create lasting impressions with their customers. There's actually some science behind what they're doing, too. It turns out emotion and memory are closely linked.

EMOTION AND MEMORY

Emotional experiences make a profound imprint on our long-term memory. We generate emotion and record memories in the limbic system, a collection of glands and structures in the brain's foldy gray matter. In his book *Brain Rules,* molecular biologist John Medina shares the science behind the relationship between emotion and memory:

> *Emotionally charged events persist much longer in our memories and are recalled with greater accuracy than neutral memories.*
>
> *How does this work in our brains? It involves the prefrontal cortex, the uniquely human part of the brain that governs "executive functions" such as problem-solving, maintaining attention, and inhibiting emotional impulses. If the prefrontal cortex is the board chairman, the cingulate gyrus is its personal assistant. The assistant provides the chairman with certain filtering functions and assists in teleconferencing with other parts of the brain—especially the amygdala, which helps create and maintain emotions. The amygdala is chock-full of the neurotransmitter dopamine, and it uses dopamine the way an office assistant uses Post-It notes. When the brain detects an emotionally charged event, the amygdala releases dopamine into the system. Because dopamine greatly aids memory and information processing, you could say the Post-It note reads "Remember this!" Getting the brain to put a chemical Post-It note on a given piece of information means that information is going to be more robustly processed. It is what every teacher, parent, and ad executive wants.*

Add us designers to that list too, Dr. Medina!

There's a very practical reason that emotion and memory are so closely coupled—it keeps us alive. We would be doomed to repeat negative experiences and wouldn't be able to consciously repeat positive experiences if we had no memory of them. Imagine eating a delicious four-pound log of bacon and not having the sense to eat another the following day. That's a life not worth living, my friend.

As babies, we build an emotional bond with our parents when we cry and our parents offer food, a fresh diaper, or a loving touch. Our parents' response triggers the limbic system to release calming neurotransmitters. As this cycle repeats, we begin to trust that our parents will respond again when we need them, and we form an emotional bond.

A similar feedback loop happens in interface design. Positive emotional stimuli can be disarming. It builds engagement with your users, which can make the design experience feel like a chat with a friend or a trusted confidant. Although the fun design and language in Wufoo's interface may seem like window dressing, it's actually a clever brain hack. It's a powerful way to build a positive memory, which increases the chance that Wufoo's users will continue to use and trust the application.

As we'll soon see, many websites and web apps are arriving at the same conclusion. They're realizing that more people sign up for their service, stay on their site, and buy more stuff if they transcend usable to create a pleasurable experience.

Designing for emotion is good for business. So says Chris Lindland, CEO of Betabrand (http://betabrand.com), proprietors of fashion wrapped in whip-smart *Onion*-esque humor (**FIG 1.6**). Betabrand has about thirty minutes of reading material plus a generous gallery of amateur action heros putting their togs to the test. That's a lot of content. Lindland actually describes Betabrand as an online magazine that happens to sell clothes. In the end, clothes are simply the artifacts of the amazing experience customers have on their site. When you wear a pair of Betabrand's Cordaround pants, not only do you enjoy a "22% lower crotch heat index," and a "16.24% lower drag coefficient," you also remember that you're part of a select group who've discovered this modern marvel of science and fashion.

There's a fun story behind every product, and Lindland knows that making people feel good can translate into sales and marketing budget savings.

> News of fun products and experiences travel far and wide online and at absolutely no cost. It tips people from "Maybe" to "Why the hell not?" Folks sense potential energy in products that are fun to talk about.

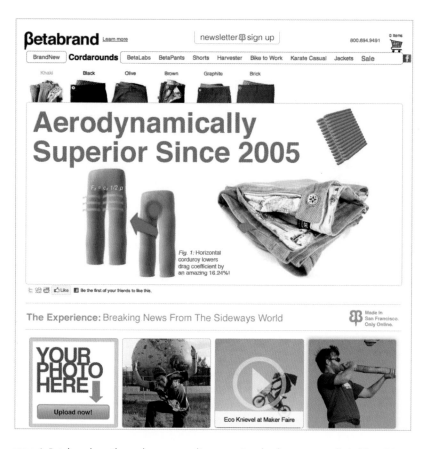

FIG 1.6: Betabrand see themselves as an online magazine that happens to sell clothing. Oh, and they can lower the drag coefficient of your crotch by an amazing 16.24%.

We'll explore the relationship between emotional design and return on investment (ROI) in Chapter 7, and even see some hard numbers. Before we get to the data, let's look at the design principle behind Betabrand's success.

THE EMOTIONAL DESIGN PRINCIPLE

They may not know it, but Betabrand has the emotional design principle at the heart of their business. When you start your next design project, keep this principle in mind: people will forgive shortcomings, follow your lead, and sing your praises if you reward them with positive emotion.

To engage your audience emotionally, you must let your brand's personality show. In the examples we've seen in Wufoo and Betabrand, personality is unmistakable. When you present your brand's personality clearly, your audience can relate to it as if it were just another human. It creates empathy and helps your audience see a better version of themselves. Humans want to connect with real people. We forget that businesses are just collections of people—so why not let that shine through?

Emotional design turns casual users into fanatics ready to tell others about their positive experience. It also offers a trust safety net that encourages your audience to stay when things go awry. Again, Chris Lindland of Betabrand reinforces this idea with a story about a customer we'll call the Pink Panther from Portland.

> A customer in Portland learned of a Cordarounds sale 10 days after buying a pair and wrote to ask for a discount. He told me companies like Nordstom offer such rebates, and I asked if a one-man online business should be held to the same standards of a multi-billion dollar biz with thousands of employees.
>
> Our disagreement was following a predictable path until I realized there was no holy way in hell he'd ever buy anything from us again, so I proposed a wager—if his Portland Trailblazers could defeat the lowly Clippers, not only would he get a discount but a pink pair of pants. If I won, I'd give him a discount and he'd have to tell two people that he's now a consultant for Betabrand.
>
> He tuned into the game with his wife, listened as the Trailblazers won, and earned himself a prized pair of Pink Panthers.
>
> To this very day, he remains one of our greatest, most loyal customers. Why? Because he found something that's better than customer service—fun customer experience.
>
> In addition to this, our greatest customer also became an investor in our company.

The Pink Panther had a bad start with Betabrand, and Lindland could have done what most of use would have: tell the guy to go fish. But Lindland changed the tone by talking to the Panther like a friend. He won a lifelong customer and an investor by staying true to his company's personality. Emotional design isn't just about copy, photos, or design style: it's a different way to think about how you communicate.

Certainly, emotional design has risks. If emotional engagement compromises the functionality, reliability, or usability of an interface, the positive experience you wanted will mutate into a rant-inducing disaster for your users. A friendly wager with an upset customer isn't always going to turn the tide.

We'll have a candid discussion about the pitfalls of emotional design and how to avoid them. But before we do, I'll help you understand the firmware that powers the human perspective, as it's the framework for the strategies you'll craft in your next project.

2

DESIGNING FOR HUMANS

WE HUMANS ARE COMPLEX BEINGS, and can be difficult to design for. We all have distinct personalities, emotional baggage, and unique dispositions, so how can we design something that can appeal to such wide-ranging perspectives?

Beneath disparate personalities and perspectives lie universal psychology principles common to all humans. These principles are invaluable tools in our quest to design for emotion. In this chapter, we'll explore the psychological firmware we share and establish a foundation on which we can build emotional design strategies.

THAT WHICH UNITES US

If there is one trait common to all humans, it is that we all emote. In *The Expression of the Emotions in Man and Animal,* Charles Darwin observed

> *The same state of mind is expressed throughout the world with remarkable uniformity; and this fact is in itself interesting as evidence of the close*

similarity in bodily structure and mental disposition of all the races of mankind.

What Darwin suggests is that we have a common emotional lexicon guiding us through life. We don't develop emotions after birth by watching others. We're born ready to express pain, joy, surprise, anger, and other emotions. Emotion is an essential survival tool. It's how we communicate our needs to our caregivers, and later in life, it's how we build beneficial relationships. Though we develop verbal language as we mature, emotion is our native tongue from the moment we enter this world. It is the lingua franca of humanity.

HUMAN NATURE AND DESIGN: BABY-FACE BIAS

We can learn a lot about design and how to communicate effectively with our audience by studying evolutionary psychology. As humans have evolved physically, so too have our brains, to naturally select the most advantageous instincts and behaviors that will keep our species alive. We call these instincts "human nature." They're the Rosetta Stone that offers insight into why we behave the way we do. Let's look at a familiar instinct and see how it may inform our design work.

Parents love their babies. If you're not a parent, you might wonder why people would want to subject themselves to sleepless nights, poopy diapers, and constant caregiving while relinquishing the freedoms and delights of adulthood. On paper, it sounds pretty bad. But in reality, it's pure magic for reasons that are hard to explain.

Shortly before I began writing this book, I became a parent. Holy cow, is it hard work! But when I see my son's face, I forget that I'm running on three hours of sleep, and that his pants are filled with unspeakables. All I see is pure beauty that is totally worth it.

Evolution has given us baby goggles that help us look past such shortcomings and trigger waves of positive emotions when we see a little one's face. The proportions of a baby's face—large eyes, small nose, pronounced forehead—are a pattern our brains recognize as very special. Faces that have such

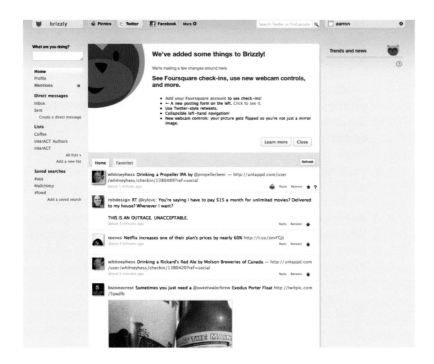

FIG 2.1: Brizzly uses the baby-face bias principle to endear their brand to their customers.

proportions are perceived as innocent, trustworthy, cute, and lovable. We're hard wired to love babies.

I know it sounds kind of crazy, but scientists believe that the original reason we evolved to love baby faces is so that we wouldn't kill them. Cuteness is a baby's first line of defense. As the late evolutionary biologist Stephen Jay Gould explains in his essay *A Biological Homage to Mickey Mouse*, cartoonists have exploited this principle for decades, creating characters with large heads, small bodies, and enlarged eyes that endear them to us.

Designers also use this principle, called the baby-face bias, to their advantage. Can you think of any websites that use a cute mascot to create connections with their audience?

There are boatloads of them. Twitter, StickyBits (http:// stickybits.com/), Brizzly (http://brizzly.com; **FIG 2.1**), and MailChimp (http://mailchimp.com) are just a few.

The takeaway here is not to make your website cuter. With a little consideration you'll discover that behind every design principle is a connection to human nature and our emotional instincts. In fact, human nature is reflected in every aspect of design.

THE WORLD IS OUR MIRROR

We humans project ourselves into so much of what we see. As we gaze at the world, we discover ourselves looking back. When we stare at the clouds, or inspect the grain of a gnarled piece of wood, inevitably we'll construct the image of a face in our mind's eye. We are accidental narcissists seeking that which we know best—ourselves.

This instinct is guided by our primordial desire for emotional connection with others. We are hardwired to seek emotion in human faces. For this reason, as we'll see in the next chapter, photos of human faces in a design can profoundly influence an audience.

We don't have to see two eyes and a mouth to feel an emotional connection to a design. Sometimes we perceive human presence through abstract things such as proportion. Pythagoras and the ancient Greeks realized this when they discovered the golden ratio, a mathematical division of proportions found repeatedly in nature, including the human form. We've used this concept for thousands of years to create art, architecture, and designs that are universally perceived to be beautiful. Though our minds may not be conscious that the golden ratio is present in architecture such as the Parthenon or in a design like the iPod, our subconscious immediately sees a pattern of beauty that we know is also present in our own bodies. If you've ever read Robert Bringhurst's brilliant book, *The Elements of Typographic Style*, you'll know that print

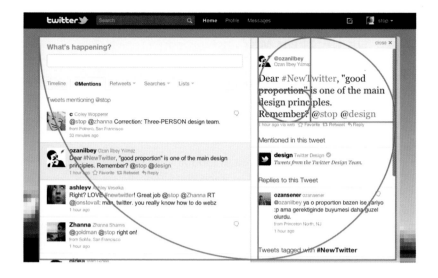

FIG 2.2: The redesign of Twitter's interface employs the golden ratio to structure page layout, making it beautiful to the human eye.

designers have used the golden ratio for centuries as the foundation of page layout.

Web designers have picked up on this concept too. When Doug Bowman and his design team at Twitter redesigned their site, the golden ratio defined the structure of the layout (**FIG 2.2**).

Our definition of beauty originates in our own image. The human mind is exceptionally skilled at scanning objects and information to discover meaning in abstract forms. We can find traces of ourselves in most anything we see, and we like that.

Our ability to find signal and discern patterns in so much noise is a very important trait we use to navigate life, and as you might expect, this ability to recognize patterns greatly affects the way we design.

CONTRAST: IS IT GOOD FOR ME
OR BAD FOR ME?

Beyond our ability to express emotion, we also share the instinct to search for patterns. The human mind is a beautifully engineered difference engine. Our brains constantly scan for patterns in our environment to form insights and keep us from harm.

Your senses alert you to food in your fridge that's past its prime. No one had to teach you about the smell of spoiled milk—you simply recognize something isn't right. Something's different and your brain knows it.

We call that break in pattern *contrast*. Our brain's vigilant scan for contrast drives our decision making process. It helps us decide where we should sit in a classroom (is one seat more advantageous than another?), where we should eat dinner (will one restaurant have better food than another?), and even who we should marry (is one mate more attractive than another?). We use contrast to answer one fundamental question: Is it good for me or bad for me?

We perceive contrast in a couple of ways:

- *Visual contrast:* difference in shape, color, form, etc.
- *Cognitive contrast:* difference in experiences or memories

Zebras' patterned hides act as visual contrast to help them blend in with a herd so that stalking lions can't pick them off. When all individuals are high contrast, none stand out.

Humans use visual contrast similarly. Habitual speeders (like me) stick close to other cars to avoid the notice of police. Speeding alone makes you an easy mark for lurking cops. (I can't say I advocate this approach, though, as two speeding tickets sit on my desk as I write.)

Police issue speeding tickets to create cognitive contrast in our minds. They hope that the penalties we incur will deter us from repeating mistakes. I can humbly attest that their technique works. It's dropped a few pounds from my lead foot.

FIG 2.3: Tumblr's cleverly simple home page limits content and effectively directs user focus.

Contrast is also a powerful design tool. It influences our users' activity in simple and profound ways. Websites like Tumblr (**FIG 2.3**) that seek new account signups improve their conversion rates by eliminating all extraneous homepage content. The site simply introduces the product and calls the user to act. The high visual contrast in negative space against the large, central form makes it easy to understand what this site is about and what action Tumblr expects.

Page simplicity also helps potential customers to perform a basic cost-benefit analysis, a regular activity that our brains engage in after contrast scanning. The short time needed to fill out the form is a low cost to pay for the potentially large benefit of the service, making conversion highly likely.

Contrast is a powerful tool, but don't overuse it, as our brains have limitations.

A LIMITED PROCESSOR

When you wield contrast effectively, as Tumblr does, interfaces become more usable too. As you increase the number of high contrast elements on a page, you proportionally increase the time needed to perform a task, learn a system, and remember pathways. Adding stuff pushes the human brain to its limits. Have you ever been to a party where everyone is yelling to speak to the person next to them? As the volume increases, everyone must speak louder to be heard, but that makes it even harder to have a conversation. Design works in the same way. If everything yells for your viewer's attention, nothing is heard.

Hick's Law is a design principle that conveys this concept. It states that the time it takes to make a decision increases with the number of alternatives. Tumblr is on to something with its dead simple home page. Though incredibly powerful, the human brain's ability to quickly parse a great deal of information is limited. It's much harder to direct a user to act if their brain has to filter noise. In that respect, we're just like the hungry lioness struggling to pinpoint the right zebra to attack.

Tumblr recognizes that attention is a finite commodity. Every time we add content to an interface, it makes it harder for humans to identify patterns and contrasting elements. The result is more unpredictable user behavior, and lower information retention. (Remind your boss of that the next time you're asked to shoehorn more stuff into your company's home page.)

But contrast doesn't just shape the way we see things: it also influences our ability to recognize abstract concepts like brands.

BRAND CONTRAST

Just as Tumblr's visual contrast helps direct user behavior, we can use cognitive contrast to shape audience perceptions. In fact, this is the primary goal of branding: to set your identity apart from your competitors'. When your brand clearly contrasts with others, your audience will easily identify it and remember it.

Web designer Ricardo Mestra gets the power of contrast. His website (http://duplos.org) defies common web design conventions (**FIG 2.4**).

Mestre's design doesn't follow a strict grid; it's organic. The rich textures, unrefined edges, and layers of flat shapes make it feel more like elegant paper craft than a website. The purple monster that darts from behind a tree and the humorous copy create an emotional imprint on his audience, making his portfolio unforgettable. When you're competing against web designers, cognitive contrast is essential.

Great design that uses cognitive and visual contrast not only makes you stand out, it can also influence the way people use your interface.

THE POWER OF AESTHETICS

Though their styles are on opposite ends of the spectrum, Tumblr and Mestre's websites have one thing in common: they're both aesthetically pleasing. Both use color, type, scale, whitespace, and layout deftly. Both are unmistakably well designed.

Design is too often wrongly taken for the indulgent frosting on a functional interface. Have you ever overheard a colleague declare, "It would be nice if we could have a sexy interface, but people care more about what the site does than how it looks"? Would this person show up to a job interview in their pajamas because people only care about what they can do and not how they look? If they did, I'd bet they'd discover that thinking is flawed.

FIG 2.4: Ricardo Mestre's web design portfolio defies convention.

Perceptions are critical. As we'll see in the coming chapters, design influences emotional engagement and usability.

As Donald Norman, a pioneer in usability and human-computer interaction, points out in his book *Emotional Design,* beautiful design creates a positive emotional response in the brain, which actually improves our cognitive abilities.

Attractive things make people feel good, which in turn makes them think more creatively. How does that make something easier to use? Simple, by making it easier for people to find solutions to the problems they encounter.

Norman is describing the aesthetic-usability effect. Attractive things actually work better.

Many brands employ this principle, but none more so than Apple.

Apple's interface design is famously refined, focused, aesthetically pleasing, and usable. Their clean, elegant design makes their products and software easy to use. Apple bakes the aesthetic-usability effect into everything they make, and it keeps their customers coming back.

But Apple fanaticism connects directly to their mastery of emotional design. When Steve Jobs concludes a product demo with "We think you're going to love it," he truly believes it. It's no mistake that he uses the word "love," as their design ethos demonstrates that Apple clearly understands human psychology and emotion.

In 2002, Apple filed a patent for a "Breathing Status LED Indicator." Anyone who owns a Mac is familiar with the status light on the front of Apple laptops and desktops that gently pulses to indicate a sleep state. Apple designers considered the context in which this light would most often be seen—in a dark office, a bedroom, or a living room where the status light is one of the only light sources.

The status indicator's pulse rate is very precise. It mimics the natural breathing rate of a human at rest: twelve to twenty breaths per minute. It works just like a gentle rhythmic pat on a baby's back. It inspires a mood. Like the Parthenon's golden proportions, a human might not correlate the light's pulse rate to their breathing rate, but they can feel its calming effect. Apple could have simply designed the indicator to stay on during sleep state, and it would have achieved its goal. Instead, their solution communicates and soothes, encouraging humans to see themselves in the product they use.

A FOUNDATION FOR EMOTIONAL DESIGN

We've discovered some design principles and common traits of the human mind in this chapter, and they'll resurface in chapters to come.

A quick look at evolutionary psychology showed us that much of how we see our world is predisposed at birth, a function of thousands of years of adapting to our environment and finding the best solutions for survival. The baby-face bias is one such example. Contrast also originates in our need to survive, but today we can use it to shape user behavior and make our brand stand out.

We learned that the human mind has limitations. When contrast is overused, we struggle to process our options, as Hick's Law dictates. And, we discovered that aesthetics is more than just window dressing—it influences usability, as the aesthetic-usability principle illustrates.

This is who we are. We are born with firmware that guides us, and emotion is at the core of that code. Emotion is a fundamental part of who we are as humans, and it plays a foundational role in effective design.

While the human use of emotion to communicate and our reactions to certain situations are universal, designing for emotion still requires nuance and careful consideration. The personalities that sit atop our cognitive firmware make us much more unpredictable. As we'll discover in the next chapter, personality is the platform for our broader emotional responses and the key to making a design more human.

3 PERSONALITY

OUR LASTING RELATIONSHIPS center around the unique qualities and perspectives we all possess. We call it personality. Through our personalities, we express the entire gamut of human emotion. Personality is the mysterious force that attracts us to certain people and repels us from others. Because personality greatly influences our decision-making process, it can be a powerful tool in design.

PERSONALITY IS THE PLATFORM FOR EMOTION

Interface design lives in a broader category called Human-Computer Interaction, or HCI, sitting among computer science, behavioral science, and design. HCI specialists understand psychology, usability, interaction design, programming concepts, and basic visual design principles. Sound familiar? That's an awful lot like what user experience designers wrangle every day.

I'll let you in on a secret. I'm not a fan of the name "Human-Computer Interaction." When I design, I work very hard to make the interface experience feel like there's a human on the other end, not a computer. It might sound like I'm splitting hairs, but names are important. Names shape our perceptions, and cue us into the ideas that fit within a category.

Emotional design's primary goal is to facilitate *human-to-human* communication. If we're doing our job well, the computer recedes into the background, and personalities rise to the surface. To achieve this goal, we must consider how we interact with one another in real life.

I'd like you to pause for a moment, and recall a person with whom you recently made a real connection. Maybe you met them while taking a walk, while at an event, or maybe a friend introduced you, and the ensuing conversation was engaging, interesting, and maybe even fun. What was it about that person that made your conversation so exhilarating? You probably had common interests that sparked discussion, but that wasn't what made the encounter so memorable, was it? It was their personality that drew you to them, that guided the discussion and left you feeling excited. Your personalities intersected in shared jokes, tone of voice, and the cadence of the conversation. This dropped your guard and made you trust this new person. Personalities foster friendships and serve as the platform for emotional connections.

Hold on to that memory, and carry it through this book. Revisit it when you start a new design project. That feeling is what we're trying to craft through emotional design. We'll create that feeling of excitement and we'll bond with our audience by designing a personality that our interface will embody.

Let's think of our designs not as a facade for interaction, but as people with whom our audience can have an inspired conversation. Products are people, too.

Once again, history can inform our work today. It turns out that designers have been experimenting with personality to craft a more human experience for centuries.

FIG 3.1: Gutenberg's movable type mimicked the calligraphic hand of a scribe in an attempt to make his mechanically produced bibles feel more human. (Source: http://bkaprt.com/de/3)

A BRIEF HISTORY OF PERSONALITY IN DESIGN

We have a history of injecting personality into the things we make, in a bid to make mechanical things more human. When Johannes Gutenberg—goldsmith and father of the printing press—experimented with movable type in the mid-fifteenth century, the human hand inspired him. Before the printing press, scribes—usually monks—painstakingly penned each page of religious manuscripts by hand with quill and ink. Transcribing a bible was a sacred duty, as the scribe was thought to be channeling a divine message. For this reason, the hand's presence in these manuscripts has great spiritual importance.

So when Gutenberg designed and cast the original typefaces he used to print hundreds of bibles, the letterforms mimicked the calligraphic style of scribes. Though he created

FIG 3.2: Personality is front and center in the Volkswagen Beetle's design, which helped to make it a smashing success through generations. (Source: http://bkaprt.com/de/4)

machines to deliver the divine message, he worked hard to make the presentation human (FIG 3.1).

We can see the trend of distinctly human design in the twentieth century, when mass production permeated nearly every industry.

The Volkswagen Beetle, released in 1938 and produced until 2003, is the best selling design in automotive history. Its distinctly human design contributed to its success (FIG 3.2). Conceived as the "People's Car," the anthropomorphized design makes it more than a car for the people: it's a car that *is* a person. The round headlights denote eyes while its scoop-shaped hood smiles at us, personifying the baby-face bias. Though originally designed for aerodynamics not personality, the Beetle's "face" conveys a perpetually hopeful and fun attitude that made it easy for generations to connect with, despite dramatic cultural changes over seven decades.

That smile that greets its driver reflects emotion and establishes a specific kind of relationship. It's hard not to return a smile even if it's coming from an object. Around that simple interaction we've constructed an emotional persona for this car, leading to games ("Slug bug red!") and the Beetle as movie hero (Herbie in *The Love Bug*). We've created memories around these experiences and they remind us of the positive emotions the Beetle inspires.

Though the Gutenberg bibles and the Volkswagen Beetle are interesting examples, there is no more concrete an example of personality in design than Apple's "Get a Mac" ad campaign. In the ads, Justin Long portrays a young hipster Mac who effortlessly tackles complex problems while his foil—John Hodgman's dweeby, uncool PC—bungles every task. These ads convey a personality experience and help consumers compare the differing relationships they could have with their computer. They don't talk about specs and features, they show how you will feel if you buy a Mac.

With a sense of the history of personality in design, let's return to the present, where you and I are working hard to understand our audience and doing our best to craft engaging web experiences.

PERSONAS

In modern web design, we research, plan, and create with our audience's attitudes and motivations in mind. User experience designers interview their audience, then create personas—a dossier on an archetypal user who represents a larger group. Think of personas as the artifacts of user research. They help a web design team remain aware of their target audience and stay focused on their needs.

The persona example shown in FIG 3.3, created by Todd Zaki Warfel, principal designer at messagefirst (http://messagefirst.com), tells the story of Julia, a certain category of user. Through this document we learn about her demographics, her interests, her expertise in various subjects, and what influences her decisions on subjects germane to the project—we start to understand who Julia is. We get a glimpse

THE INFLUENCER

Julia

Age: 19 - 22; Sophomore; Journalism & Communications

Goals: Get a "Big City College" education, cosmopolitan experience; Build resume with internship; Take new/different courses; Make new/different friends; Experience different cultures

Pain Points: Limited courses offered; Costs; Organization (too much or not enough); Advantages are hidden; Challenging to transfer credits

My internship provided me with the opportunity to work in Times Square. I just love all of the lights, action, and excitement!

Julia has been taking Spanish since high school and is excited to study abroad in Buenos Aires next spring. She's traveled a little in the past—to Great Britain for a vacation with her family and to Mexico for a missions trip—but this is her first time going abroad alone. Though she has other friends who also plan to study abroad, she wanted to go at a different time so she would be forced to make friends with the locals and truly immerse herself in the culture. She's heard from friends that the maturity level of some of the students plummets the moment they step on the plane to study abroad. She hopes they don't make her look like a "stupid American."

She's also heard that the dorms in Buenos Aires aren't great, which solidified her decision to do a homestay. However, she's concerned about commuting to classes, which she hopes to take at the NYU campus as well as a local university—if the credits transfer. She doesn't have a lot of extra cash and is interested in a work study to pay for souvenirs and some travel around Argentina. Speaking Spanish on the job would also be great practice, but she isn't sure what sort of opportunities there are, or even if she's allowed to work.

Knowledge

Lifecycle

Activities and Interest

Influencers

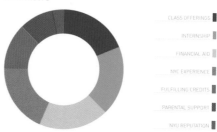

messagefirst | design studio

FIG 3.3: Personas help guide the design process, keeping the focus on user needs.

of her personality, which helps us to understand her motivations and shapes the design decisions that follow.

Although Julia is not a real person, but an archetypal representative of a user group, she's actually closely based on a person that the folks at messagefirst know. They create all of their personas this way, which is handy. When they encounter a tricky point in their design process where they're unsure of which perceptions, values, and behaviors to expect of their audience in a specific interface, they can simply phone them and ask questions. Not only does this help them create better design solutions, it keeps them focused on real people who will use the things they make.

As we saw in the hierarchy of needs in Chapter 1, we know all users need our designs to be functional, reliable, and usable. By understanding our audience, we can better address their needs. This information also helps us address the top layer in that hierarchy—pleasure—by clueing us in to the design personality most likely to create an emotional connection.

Personas are a standard tool in the design process, but they only provide a partial picture of the relationship we're building with our audience. We know who they are, but who are we? Earlier in the chapter I mentioned that products can be people too. Following that line of thinking, shouldn't our design have a persona that serves as the foil for our user personas? Why, yes—yes it should.

CREATING A DESIGN PERSONA FOR YOUR WEBSITE

If your website were a person, who would it be? Is it serious, buttoned up, all business, yet trustworthy and capable? Is it a wise-cracking buddy that makes even mundane tasks fun?

Following a structure similar to a user persona, you can flesh out your design's personality by creating a design persona. Personality can manifest itself in an interface through visual design, copy, and interactions. A design persona describes how to channel personality in each of these areas and helps the web team to construct a unified and consistent result. The goal is to construct a personality portrait every bit as clear as those Justin Long and John Hodgman convey in the "Get a Mac" ads.

Before we take a look at a real design persona I created for MailChimp, let's examine the components of the document. Here's what you'll include in your design persona:

Brand name: The name of your company or service.

Overview: A short overview of your brand's personality. What makes your brand personality unique?

Personality image: This is an actual image of a person that embodies the traits you wish to include in your brand. This makes the personality less abstract. Pick a famous person, or a person with whom your team is familiar. If your brand has a mascot or representative that already embodies the personality, use that instead. Describe the attributes of the mascot that communicate the brand's personality.

Brand traits: List five to seven traits that best describe your brand along with a trait that you want to avoid. This helps those designing and writing for this design persona to create a consistent personality while avoiding the traits that would take your brand in the wrong direction.

Personality map: We can map personalities on an X / Y axis. The X axis represents the degree to which the personality is unfriendly or friendly; the Y axis shows the degree of submissiveness or dominance.

Voice: If your brand could talk, how would it speak? What would it say? Would it speak with a folksy vernacular or a refined, erudite clip? Describe the specific aspects of your brand's voice and how it might change in various communication situations. People change their language and tone to fit the situation, and so should your brand's voice.

Copy examples: Provide examples of copy that might be used in different situations in your interface. This helps writers understand how your design persona should communicate.

Visual lexicon: If you are a designer creating this document for yourself and/or a design team, you can create a visual lexicon in your design persona that includes an overview of the colors, typography, and visual style that conveys your brand's personality. You can be general about these concepts, or include a mood board (http://bkaprt.com/de/5).

Engagement methods: Describe the emotional engagement methods you might use in your interface to support the design persona and create a memorable experience. We'll learn more about these in the next chapter.

Now we'll take a look at a real-world example. As the user experience design lead at MailChimp, I created a design persona to guide the work we do. Following the same structure as we've just seen, here's a slightly abbreviated version of the document we use:

Brand name: MailChimp

Overview: Freddie Von Chimpenheimer IV is the face of MailChimp and the embodiment of the brand personality (**FIG 3.5**). Freddie's stout frame communicates the power of the application, and his on-the-go posture lets people know this brand means business.

Freddie always has a kind smile that welcomes users and makes them feel at home. The cartoon style communicates that MailChimp offers a fun and informal experience. Yes, he's a cartoon ape, but somehow Freddie can still be cool. He likes to crack witty jokes, but when the situation is serious, the funny business stops.

MailChimp often surprises users with a fun easter egg, or a link to a gut-busting YouTube video. Fun is around every corner, but never in the way of the workflow.

Personality image: FIG 3.4

Brand traits: Fun, but not childish. Funny, but not goofy. Powerful, but not complicated. Hip, but not alienating. Easy, but not simplistic. Trustworthy, but not stodgy. Informal, but not sloppy.

Personality map: FIG 3.5

Voice: MailChimp's voice is familiar, friendly, and—above all—human. The personalities of the people behind the brand shine through honestly. The voice of MailChimp cracks jokes (ones you can share with your mama), tells stories, and communicates with the folksy tone that you might use with an old friend. MailChimp uses contractions like "don't" instead of "do not" because that's how real humans speak to one another. MailChimp uses sound effects like, "hmmmmm...." to make it sound like you're thinking hard, or "Blech, that's awful!" to communicate empathy. Lowercase form and button text reinforce the brand's informality.

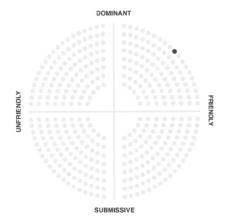

FIG 3.5: MailChimp's personality map.

Copy examples: *Success message*: "High fives! Your list has been imported." *Error message*: "Oops, looks like you forgot to enter an email address." *Critical failure*: "One of our servers is temporarily down. Our engineers are already on the case and will have it back online shortly. Thanks for your patience."

Visual lexicon: *Color*: MailChimp's bright yet slightly desaturated color palette conveys a sense of fun and humor. The colors feel refined—not romper room-y. MailChimp is fun, but it's also powerful. *Typography*: MailChimp is easy-going, efficient, and easy to use, and its typography reflects it. Simple, sans-serif headings and body copy vary appropriately in scale, weight, and color to communicate information hierarchy, making MailChimp feel like a familiar, comfortable cardigan that is both functional and beloved. *General style notes*: Interface elements are flat and simple, keeping things easy to understand and unintimidating. Soft, subtle textures may appear in places to warm up the space and make it feel human. Freddie should be used sparingly, and only to interject a bit of humor. Freddie never gives application feedback, stats, or helps with a task.

Engagement methods: *Surprise and delight*: Themed login screens commemorate holidays, cultural events, or a beloved individual. Easter eggs create unexpected moments of humor that may convey nostalgia or reference kitschy pop culture. *Anticipation*: Freddie's random funny greetings at the top of each main page create anticipation for the next page to load. These greetings never provide information or feedback. They are a fun layer that never interferes with functionality or usability.

Download a design persona template and the MailChimp example at http://aarronwalter.com/design-personas. Try it on your next project, or maybe even on a redesign.

Just as user experience designers post personas in a place where the design, development, and content strategy teams will see them throughout the project, your design persona should be visible to remind the team of the type of relationship you want to build with your audience. The design persona should guide anyone that crafts a pixel, a paragraph, or a process on your website.

Many websites are already using personality to shape the user experience and power their commercial success. Though dissimilar in brand, business goals, and platform, Tapbots, Carbonmade, and Housing Works have discovered that personality is the key ingredient in the emotional connections they're building with their audience and in their overwhelming success.

Tapbots: robot love

Tapbots (http://tapbots.com), makers of handy little iPhone apps, have created a distinct personality in their interfaces, making otherwise nerdy tasks seem enjoyable (**FIG 3.6**).

The Convertbot app, as its name foretells, simply converts between various units of measure. The Weightbot app helps users track fluctuations in body weight. Neither of these tasks is terribly enjoyable to perform, especially weight tracking, which can rattle your self-esteem. But the apps' design has created a loyal following that's made them a smashing success.

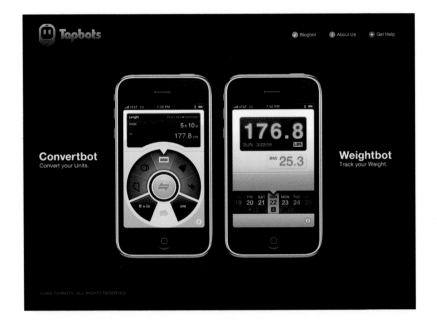

FIG 3.6: The Tapbots apps feel like lovable little robots ready to do your number-crunching dirty work.

The apps seem to have faces through which all interaction takes place. The dark panels at the top resemble Kool Moe Dee-inspired sunglasses propped above a slight triangle nose and a broad mouth. If you must track your weight, a cyborg Kool Moe Dee is a good partner in crime.

Unlike other iPhone apps, the interfaces seem like little human robots. One robot in particular inspired Tapbots app designer Mark Jardine to design personality into the user interface:

> The whole UI concept was really inspired by the movie, WALL·E. Our concept for the first two apps was to design them as if they were physical robots.
>
> We want our apps to be used seriously, but also give the sense that they are more than just a piece of software. We want our

users to have an emotional connection to our apps. Most people don't have a love/joy for software like geeks do.

Users react with effusive emotion to these cartoony, yet seemingly tangible interfaces enhanced by robotic whirs, bleeps, and blips. You can certainly see the parallels with WALL·E, in physical and personality traits. Both are friendly, endearing, and reliable.

Technology blogger John Gruber sums up audience sentiment about Tapbots apps with this simple review (http://bkaprt.com/de/6):

I adore the way their apps look and sound.

Ironically, Gruber doesn't even mention the apps' functionality, though his appreciation of it is implied. He uses the word "adore." Gruber doesn't just like these apps; he *loves* them. These anthropomorphized interfaces give users the sense that they are interacting with another living being with a personality, making an emotional connection possible. Interfaces that can tap into emotion effectively not only create a broad fan base, they build an army of evangelists.

The brand personality train chugs on in the next example. Carbonmade manages to construct an effective brand personality that resonates with their audience while bathing in a sea of mustachioed wackiness.

Carbonmade: octopi, unicorns, and mustachios

Personality can forge relationships with an audience only to the extent that it's unique and authentic. If it's used as a gimmick, it can have the opposite effect. As we saw in Chapter 2, our brains are hardwired to detect things that are good for us or bad for us. People will notice contrived, inauthentic personality in a design, which will send them packing and ensure that they'll never trust your brand.

Carbonmade (http://carbonmade.com), a clever little web app that helps people design elegant portfolios, expresses their personality throughout their site, combining the earnestness

FIG 3.7: Carbonmade uses an over-the-top personality to woo new users to their service.

of Jimmy Stewart with Eddie Izzard's exploding, goofy charm. Octopi and unicorns frolic in their fantastical homepage landscape (**FIG 3.7**)—atypical for a conversion-focused site.

This quirky personality and tongue-in-cheek humor is conjured by their designer Dave Gorum, and as it turns out, it's what encourages skeptical designers and artists to sign up. Gorum explains:

> *My rule was and is to add fun up to the point that it distracts from the message.*
>
> *Keeping things informal and bonkers makes it all the easier to get folks to click that sign-up button. There's a taper to the silliness though. We lay it on pretty thick in our marketing site, dial it back a bit in our admin tools, and remove it all together on the product. It's like a giant, flashy, goofy piece of candy on the outside, with a Swiss-engineered, straight-laced nougaty center!*

Carbonmade's humor and personality is like a reverse mullet: party up front, and business in the back. Dialing back the over-the-top personality in their application allows users to focus on workflow rather than getting lost in a sea of mustaches, a point that we'll discuss further in Chapters 4 and 7. The informal tone of the product site, however, creates a rapport that makes the audience feel comfortable with subscribing to the service, while misdirecting competitors who may believe that Carbonmade is all frivolity and no substance:

> *The informality makes it super easy to open a dialogue with our audience. We're like their goofy friend who's really easy to talk to and can make them a sweet portfolio.*
>
> *If anything, the smirking goofiness lets our competitors feel comfortable about not taking us seriously. Which is juuuuust fine.*

Carbonmade's brand personality creates clear contrast for an audience that's trying to compare them to the competition. As we saw in Chapter 2, contrast is an essential part of the human decision making process.

FIG 3.8: Housing Works builds an emotional bond with its audience by sharing the stories of the amazing people it serves.

While humor is in the wheelhouse of Carbonmade's personality, it's not always appropriate. It's our desire to share a bit of our selves with others that shapes the personality in our designs, and helps us to connect with our audience. We're all complex people with a broad range of emotions. When it comes to emotional design, we need to tailor the personality to the content and audience.

Few websites do this as well as Housing Works, which puts a human face on an important cause.

Housing Works: a name with a face

As is true in the real world, we can't always punctuate site personalities with wit and humor. Certain situations call for a different tactic.

Housing Works (http://housingworks.org) is an inspiring non-profit dedicated to ending AIDS and homelessness.

Housing Works changes lives every day. Their story is one of empathy, kindness, and hope for everyday people.

When Happy Cog (http://happycog.com) redesigned Housing Works' website in 2008 (**FIG 3.9**), the personalities of the organization and the people it serves were the muses of their design process.

Dan Mall, the Housing Works design lead, explains:

It was very clear that the heart of Housing Works is the people that serve and people that it serves. It was overwhelmingly about warmth and care. Under that direction, it was easy to design the site you see today.

Large photographs and quotes about how Housing Works has changed a life figure prominently on the homepage, communicating the organization's personality while inspiring their audience. Smiling faces and personal stories cycle softly, helping the site to achieve real human-to-human communication.

Photo cropping shapes the audience's emotional perspective. The face-ism ratio design principle states that photographs cropped tight to the subject's face encourage an emotional response from the viewer, while emphasizing the personality of the subject. Wider subject cropping emphasizes the physical appearance of the subject. Photos on the Housing Works homepage are cropped perfectly to help us see the beautiful personalities of the people depicted, making us sympathetic to their cause.

THE POWER OF PERSONALITY

Just as our personalities shift with the context of communication in real life, they must shift in the projects we design. There's no one-size-fits-all solution. If we stop thinking of the interfaces we design as dumb control panels, and think of them as the people our target audience wants to interact with, we can craft emotionally engaging experiences that make a lasting impression.

Keep in mind that when you emphasize personality in the user experience, some people won't like it. That's okay, though. Personalities clash, and in the case of businesses, it can actually be a good thing. If people don't understand your personality, chances are they're not the right customer for you, and you're actually saving yourself future customer-relations problems. As we'll see in Chapter 7, personality is a risk, but there are many real-world examples that suggest the rewards are worth it.

With personality as the foundation of your designs, you can layer more emotional engagement on top, as we'll discover in the coming chapter.

4 EMOTIONAL ENGAGEMENT

AS WE'VE SEEN IN CHAPTER 3, personality is by itself a powerful way to engage your audience. It helps people understand who you are and shapes how they interact with you, while setting the tone for the voice, aesthetic, and interaction design of your site.

The design persona we created in Chapter 3 was the blueprint for emotional design. Now we're ready to use that foundation and start building concrete interaction patterns that harness the power of psychology to create positive, long-lasting memories of your site in your audience's minds.

Life itself can teach us as we examine our own emotional responses. How do we react in moments of surprise, anticipation, or when something is withheld from us? How do you feel when your status is elevated among your peers, or when someone tells you that you must do something? These situations make a lasting impression, which means a closer look could teach us how to apply emotional design.

SURPRISE AND DELIGHT

Have you ever noticed that hearing your favorite song on the radio seems so much more enjoyable than when you play it yourself? Surprise amplifies our emotional response. When we anticipate a moment, the emotional response is diluted across time. A moment of surprise compresses emotion into a split second, making our reaction more intense, and creating a strong imprint on our memory.

In Chapter 2 we learned that our brains scan for pattern breaks to identify contrasting visual and cognitive elements so we that we can react appropriately. When we're surprised, we're experiencing a high contrast situation in which something is not as we expected. A moment of surprise frames our attention, which blurs peripheral elements, and brings the extraordinary into focus.

This is a handy tool that interface designers can use to direct attention and shape user behavior. We know that people using websites and applications navigate and process content quickly and that their attention is limited. Introducing surprise into an interface can break a behavior pattern and force the brain to reassess the situation.

Surprise is always followed by a proportional emotional response. After the brain detects a surprising contrast, it has to figure out how to respond quickly. There's not enough time for deep, intellectual contemplation, so the brain relies on emotion to provide a "gut reaction." Interface designers love creating this sort of response in users because, if done well, surprise that triggers the right gut reaction bypasses cerebral judgements that might prevent users from clicking, signing up for a service, or buying. But keep in mind, our goal here is not to deceive or trick. Your audience will catch on to your game and will not trust your brand if you are deceitful. We want to build positive perceptions of our brand to create lasting brand loyalty.

Photojojo has mastered surprise's cognitive kung fu, inspiring delight and fueling their commercial success.

FIG 4.1: Photojojo's shopping cart pouts until shoppers add an item, which makes it smile in delight.

Photojojo: attack of the helpful muppets

Photojojo (http://photojojo.com)—a website devoted to making digital photography more fun—weaves surprise into their ecommerce experience. As the web has matured, ecommerce interaction design has become very standardized because it makes the purchase process easier for people to learn and remember. But Photojojo revamped the typical shopping cart interaction pattern by creating a clever moment of surprise that makes their customers want to keep shopping.

Atop each Photojojo product page perches a shopping cart with a real personality. He's gray and sullen, though at first we don't know why (**FIG 4.1**). The mystery is solved when the customer clicks the "add to cart" button, sending an item arcing across the page into the cart. The poor soul promptly turns green and smiles in delight. As it turns out, he's only happy when he's got a belly full of the products you want to buy.

Photojojo's novel shopping cart design surprises first-time visitors because it's unlike any they've seen, focusing attention on the delightful interaction that follows when they add an item to the cart. Users want to experience that moment of delight again, so they'll add more items to the cart. That's exactly what Photojojo wants customers to do.

This same surprise and delight pattern happens elsewhere on product pages. A mysterious lever sits between the "add to cart" button and the main product image. It wards off user meddling with the label "Do Not Pull." It's odd and surprising to see anything on a web page telling us *not* to interact with it. Only the most disciplined shoppers can resist such temptation. Those that pull the lever are startled as an orange, muppet-like arm descends onto the page, yanking it upward to reveal the product description, which lies below the proverbial page fold (**FIG 4.2**).

A simple "product description" link would have helped users discover this detailed information they may have otherwise missed, but the mysterious lever with its reverse psychology gets more people to read the description, and, according to Photojojo founder Amit Gupta, actually improves their conversion rates. Brilliant!

The entire site is peppered with gems that make the site fun and keep their audience coming back. Gupta describes how emotional design has broadened their audience and influenced their success:

> *Emotional design is part of our marketing strategy. People tell their friends about the bubble that hops up to the top of the page when you add something to the cart, they tell their Twitter followers and blog readers about the "Do Not Pull" lever on our product pages, they mention how much they love the sandwich and dinosaur on our contact page when they email us, and they upload photos of their invoice to their Flickr accounts. All of it works together (along with awesome products and customer*

FIG 4.2: A muppet-like arm descends from above yanking the page up when users pull the lever labeled "Do Not Pull."

service) to make the company worth talking about, and draw in new fans, customers, and friends.

A pleasant surprise is around every corner in Photojojo, and that makes customers want to keep searching for the next moment of delight. The more Photojojo encourages movement, the more products will be seen, and that helps keep sales rolling in. For Photojojo, surprise and delight are central to their success.

Remember Wufoo from Chapter 1, who helped introduce us to the idea of emotional design? Let's look at how they leave surprises for customers not in the interface, but in their real, physical mailboxes.

Wufoo: a surprisingly personal message

Surprise needn't be limited to the online experience. As we discovered in Chapter 1, Wufoo is skilled at creating emotionally engaging interactions inside their web application, but they also deliver surprises to their users' mailboxes (the old school kind of mailbox). Though hundreds of thousands of people use their app, the guys that run Wufoo pen personal letters by hand to each of their customers thanking them for their loyalty. In the age of automation and electronic communication, a personal letter from a real person at a company serving thousands of customers is as rare as finding a prancing miniature unicorn in your mailbox. It shows a care and consideration that takes recipients off guard when they open their mailbox to discover an authentic, human communiqué from the designer or developer behind a beloved web app (FIG 4.3).

These letters put a human face on the Wufoo brand. Their surprise arrival triggers a warm response from recipients who feel special in the eyes of the people at Wufoo. That feeling in

FIG 4.3: The makers of Wufoo hand-write letters to their customers. Photo courtesy of Wufoo user, Andrew Hyde (andrewhy.de).

turn triggers one consistent behavior—a web-wide broadcast to anyone who will listen. Though not meant as a marketing ploy, these letters steadily stream through Twitter, Facebook, and Flickr, making a lasting impression on people who are not yet customers, but who are much more likely to become customers because of the personal attention they see their friends receiving.

Aside from being the right thing to do, surprising people with kindness and individual attention can help a business achieve success. Wufoo has discovered that when you create emotionally engaging experiences, a marketing budget is no longer necessary. (Yes, you read that correctly: they have eliminated their marketing budget.) Their audience does the marketing for them.

Surprise's close cousin, anticipation, also holds great power. One website in particular used anticipation to shape perceptions of a looming redesign to build excitement and soften potential backlash. Which site was it? Read on to find out. (See what I did there?)

ANTICIPATION, THE VELVET ROPE, AND STATUS

Though surprise can help users by compressing emotion into a split-second reaction, anticipation—surprise's temporal opposite—can also shape emotional engagement. We create anticipation when we foreshadow a desired event and give the audience ample time to ponder the experience. Parents excite their children at Christmas with "Santa is coming to our house soon!" to conjure fantasies about the magic of the holidays and the wonderful gifts to come.

Anticipation is what game designers call an open system. Games designed with an open structure, like The Sims, allow users to wander and shape game play on their own terms. Open systems encourage people to use their imagination to create a personalized experience. Video games that use a closed system, like Super Mario Brothers, narrowly direct game play, forcing the user to move in a specific direction on a defined mission. The contrast between open and closed systems is what leads us so often to perceive that reading the book is better than seeing the movie. Books require our imagination to tell the story, but movies do all the imagining for us.

Anticipation has a similar open system effect that encourages us to use our imagination to form an image of upcoming events. Creating anticipation has a much greater influence on people than simply laying out the details, as tantalizing uncertainty leaves the mind to play in a manner most relevant to the individual. Something special awaits at the end of our anticipation, which creates a powerful yearning to end the mystery and see if the outcome meets our expectations.

The popular social networking platform Twitter used anticipation's emotional power to prime user perceptions of a pending redesign. By foreshadowing the design, then slowly rolling it out to their customers, they created a frenzy of positive conversation and emotional engagement that made it one of the most successful redesigns on the modern web.

New Twitter

In early 2010, the folks at Twitter were working on a major redesign dubbed simply "New Twitter." Doug Bowman, Twitter's creative director, pored over design concepts with his team, scrutinizing every visual detail and interaction pattern. Twitter's design researcher, Mark Trammell, conducted usability tests on the interface while it was still in development. They piped the usability test video feed into the design studio so that Bowman and his team could refine and improve the design on the fly.

With hundreds of millions of users for whom Twitter was a central part of daily life, the stakes of the redesign were high. Twitter was facing a particularly difficult launch because the fervent use of their service had ingrained each button, link, and heading in users' minds. Changes, no matter how insignificant, would be noticed.

Word of the redesign project hit the web when Bowman leaked a partial screenshot (FIG 4.4) on Dribbble (http://bkaprt.com/de/7), a site that lets designers share a tiny glimpse of what they're working on in a 400×300 pixel image. The limitations Dribbble places on screenshot size let Bowman share

FIG 4.4: Doug Bowman leaked a partial screenshot of the redesign of Twitter on Dribbble in April of 2010, sparking frenzied speculation about the project.

a fragment of the design without, as he said, "giving away the farm." It also left much to the imagination, sparking speculation about the interface lurking just outside of the preview frame.

Within minutes, the screenshot traveled around the web. Articles on *GigaOm* and *Mashable* incited hundreds of thousands of people to wonder what was in store for New Twitter. After five months of anticipation, New Twitter began to slowly roll out to a few select users. Some were well known influencers while others appeared to be chosen at random. At long last, the wait was over!

FIG 4.5: The outcome of Twitter's 2010 redesign.

Early recipients of New Twitter (**FIG 4.5**) bragged to their followers that they'd won the Twitter lottery, tagging their tweets with #NewTwitter, which created an easy-to-follow conversation around the redesign. Though the slow rollout was motivated more by a desire to mitigate any unintended consequences on infrastructure and user experience, the limited access created a velvet rope effect that had a powerful emotional influence. Users who were granted early access felt a sense of exclusivity and elevated status, which was heightened when they tweeted about it and received longing @replies from their followers.

The anticipation, exclusivity, and elevation in status for New Twitter users shaped perceptions of the new design.

@stephenpdiesel
Stephen Diesel

#newtwitter is so effing sexy.

28 Sep via web ☆ Favorite ⤸ Retweet ↶ Reply
from University, Blacksburg

@leiandroid
Leia

Omg, the #newtwitter is
AWESOOMME!!!! :D

24 Sep via web ☆ Favorite ⤸ Retweet ↶ Reply

FIG 4.6: A small sample of the positive sentiment that followed the release of New Twitter.

Though there certainly were vocal critics, the predominant perception was that New Twitter was better than its predecessor (**FIG 4.6**). Users arrived at New Twitter already feeling good, making it easier for them to enjoy the myriad design and functionality improvements. Tweets like these from early adopters primed many others to fall in love with the new design even before they had access to it.

Saying "you may" instead of "you must"

Twitter did something particularly interesting with the release. Rather than simply forcing people to switch to the new interface when they were selected, they gave everyone the option to stick with the old design if they wanted to. Giving users the power to choose changes the tone of their response. When forced to change, people often react negatively. Allow people to change on their own schedule, and you empower them, diffusing animosity. We'd all rather hear "You may..." instead of "You must...."

By contrast, Twitter's rival, Facebook, has had much less success in releasing interface revisions, because they force users to change on Facebook's schedule. When you're in a hurry and visit Facebook to briefly catch up with a friend, changes in the interface leave you feeling like someone has moved your cheese. By giving users a link to switch back to the old interface, Twitter allowed their users to feel in control. It's an open-system approach to a tricky situation that prepares people to embrace change.

As we'll soon see, shaping the user's mood before they begin important task flows can greatly improve the user experience.

PRIMING

In all of the examples we've seen, positive emotional experiences train users to fall in love with a product or service. Though the methods vary, the outcome is the same—each audience is deeply engaged. There's a common psychological principle at work here: it's called priming.

Priming happens when a person is exposed to a stimulus that in turn shapes their response to another stimulus. For example, we saw this with Photojojo's humorous site interactions, which improve their conversion rate by layering positive interactions on the pathway to purchase. These moments of surprise and delight prime user perceptions, making the site more relatable and easier to trust.

By releasing a screenshot on Dribbble, New Twitter built anticipation and suspense, which primed a successful launch. Limited access made early invitees feel special, priming their perception of the redesigned interface. That in turn encouraged effusive tweets priming the perceptions of those who had yet to gain access. It was a brilliantly effective chain of positive priming events.

Priming works by activating parts of your memory with an initial stimulus so that when a second stimulus follows, your brain is more likely to build associations. I discovered the benefit of priming user perceptions purely by accident in experiments that had interesting outcomes I never intended.

MailChimp: accidental priming

I stumbled on priming's power accidentally as the user experience design lead at MailChimp. In 2008, we did a major redesign, rebuilding most of the application. With a fun brand (we've got a chimp mascot, afterall) and unprecedented design freedom, we had a lot of leeway to test emotional design strategies.

We started small with one conspicuous, but unobtrusive element—a talking chimp at the top of select pages in the app. Freddie Von Chimpenheimer IV, as he's known by some, peeks out from the page header and delivers random, witty greetings and occasionally refers to hilarious YouTube videos (FIG 4.7). Because we knew that talking mascots have a rough history in software design, we set strict ground rules for Freddie from the beginning.

Remember Mr. Clippy, the cartoon assistant in Microsoft Office from 1997 to 2003? He inspired uncontained vitriol from users because of his poor timing. While writing a letter in Word, Clippy would slide onto the screen and ask, "It looks like you're writing a letter. Would you like help?" The general response people had was, "Get the hell out of my way you bloody pain in my backside." (That's the polite version.) Blocking a busy user's workflow is always a bad idea.

Clippy was our anti-inspiration. We wanted to achieve the opposite of what he did in Microsoft Office. We never wanted Freddie to provide feedback about the app, deliver stats, or tell you when something has gone wrong. He's not there to help. He's simply a layer of fun that enhances a usable workflow, and above all, he has to stay out of the way of our busy users.

Because his greetings are randomized, there's a little surprise awaiting users around every corner of the app.

We had a blast coming up with ridiculous greetings. Initially, we did it to entertain ourselves. Sure, we recognized

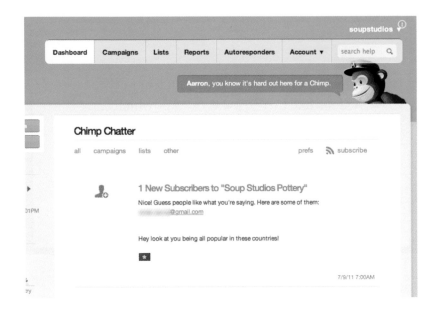

FIG 4.7: Freddie Von Chimpenheimer IV greets users and cracks jokes, making the mundane task of sending emails a little more enjoyable.

humor as an important part of our brand that sets us apart from our competition, and we wanted to let our personality shine in the app experience. But the truth is, it was fun to write copy for a talking primate and we were just a touch self-indulgent.

When we launched the new version of the app, we discovered curious things about Freddie's influence on the user experience. At first we saw tweets (FIG 4.8) about how his greetings brightened the work day.

But what really surprised and excited us was that the random jokes actually helped users complete long, more complicated task flows (FIG 4.9).

Freddie was, in fact, a cheerleader for the user, tempting them forward with a new joke on the next page. We found that just as good design improves how users perceive interface

@rdcezar
Roman Cezar

I love @mailchimp. They link you to videos like http://ow.ly/2PJqK which can make a tiring day better!

6 Oct via HootSuite ☆ Unfavorite ↱ Retweet ↰ Reply

Mentioned in this Tweet

MailChimp MailChimp ✓
MailChimp is a powerful, easy-to-use email marketing service. You design, me deliver.

FIG 4.8: MailChimp users are quick to share their reaction to Freddie's comments on Twitter.

usability (see Chapter 2 for discussion of the aesthetic-usability effect), an emotionally engaging interface can have the same effect. Varying greetings on each page kept a cheerful momentum in the workflow that helped people overcome obstacles and accomplish their goals.

When rewards like the funny little greetings arrive on a regular schedule, with varying degrees of delight, it inspires curiosity in people to see what the next reward will be. Maybe the next one will be really great? I've got to go see!

This is a psychological phenomenon called variable rewards. We recognize it as the driving force behind slot machines. People love to play slots because the big win might be waiting behind the next lever pull. Popular deal sites like Groupon (http://groupon.com) and Scoutmob (http://scoutmob.com/) use variable rewards, too. Every morning, email subscribers open their inbox wondering what great discount awaits them. Sometimes it's awesome, sometimes it's not. The uncertainty of the rewards coming on a regular

@p_girl
Leah Ford

Oh MailChimp monkey. Just as I get frustrated w/ wrangling email addresses, you're there w/ your little witticisms to cheer me up.

11 Nov 09 via web ☆ Unfavorite ⇄ Retweet ↰ Reply

FIG 4.9: Freddie's humor had a surprising affect on task flow completion rates.

schedule keeps people excited, as they anticipate what might come next.

Freddie's ever-changing jokes hold the same power. The uncertainty of what the next joke will be uses the power of variable rewards to encourage users on to the next step in their workflow, a wonderful outcome we hadn't anticipated.

As we experimented with the greetings, we introduced some that referenced specific user traits. We were hoping, like a Vegas casino boss playing the odds, that sooner or later a targeted greeting would land on just the right person, and the influence would intensify. One greeting commented on the user's haircut, which drew some mystified tweets when we displayed it at just the right time (**FIG 4.10**).

There was no way for us to know when this greeting would be most appropriate, but that's not Kate's perception. Because this greeting so perfectly coincided with her real life, it seemed to Kate that a real person was sitting behind the scenes talking to her directly. In this situation, the application had transformed from a mindless block of code into a living, breathing personality able to forge a human connection. To Kate, it felt like real human-to-human communication.

Serendipity hasn't always worked to our advantage. There have been times when greetings aligned with a user's real life uncomfortably. One greeting joked about how Freddie's tiny

@katemiss
Kate Miss

Whoa, I just logged into MailChimp and the little monkey in the corner says "hey Kate, new haircut? !Muy guapo!" how do they know?!

16 Jan 10 via web   ☆ Unfavorite ⇄ Retweet ↰ Reply

FIG 4.10: A comment from Freddie about a user's haircut won't always apply, but when it does it makes quite an impression.

little hat makes his "bum look big." Some people read it as a comment on their physical appearance, prompting a few outraged messages to the support team. In those cases, the user's mind was primed to read all butt-size commentary as a reflection on them. There's no way we could have known that, but it has made us think more carefully about the unintended consequences each greeting can have.

As we'll discover in Chapter 7, there is a certain risk to applying emotional design when speaking to a broad audience. Some people will react positively to personality and others will not. But we've discovered that the risk of some negative reactions is worth the payoff. The good will we cultivate through the greetings far outweighs the few negative responses. Freddie's greetings are, in fact, priming users to perceive the app as fun, usable, and trustworthy, which was the intended effect.

We realized how effective priming was when we saw a shift in the tone customers used when speaking with our support team. People channel their inner Freddie, cracking jokes and using banana puns. The priming effect is that "MailChimp is funny, so when I talk to MailChimp, I should be funny too." Of course, our customer service team prefers to work with a customer who is in a good mood and has a sense of humor over a sourpuss waiting to take out their frustrations on an unwitting support expert.

The greetings' priming effect doesn't just benefit customers: it benefits us, as well. We can more easily help people troubleshoot problems when they are in a positive frame of mind, shortening the average support cycle. Freddie's greetings brighten the day not just for our customers, but for us, too.

THERE IS NO FORMULA

There are common strategies we can use to design for emotional engagement. Surprise, delight, anticipation, elevating perceived status, and limiting access to elicit a feeling of exclusivity can all be effective in getting your audience to fall in love with your brand. But your tactics must be appropriate for your audience and brand experience. There is no formula for emotional design, only principles of psychology and human nature to guide you. The examples in this chapter are not meant to be emulated, only to get you thinking about how you can convey your brand personality in your interfaces in a way that resonates with your audience.

There will be times where you get it wrong, but that's okay. You can adjust to correct your course. Start small with simple interaction patterns that use some of these ideas, and see how your audience reacts. When you hit your mark, the benefits are big.

As we exit this chapter inspired by sites like Photojojo, which use humor to create an endearing personality, I'd like to interject a sobering note. There are some situations in which a light, informal tone is inappropriate. What do you do if you work on a banking site that needs to inspire trust and overcome skepticism? And even if a bit of humor is appropriate for your site, what do you do if your audience is simply apathetic to your message?

These are real challenges, but emotional design can help, as we'll see in the next chapter.

5 OVERCOMING OBSTACLES

THE LAST CHAPTER may have left you feeling warm and fuzzy about designing for emotion. It's all jokes and monkeys, right? The brute reality is that not all brand personalities afford the liberal use of humor. There are times where we need to appeal to different emotions that inspire confidence and trust in our audience.

As we discovered in Chapter 2, our brains break up complex situations into simple concepts so we can evaluate the costs and benefits of a decision. To protect ourselves from harm, we're pre-programmed to be skeptical of new brands, products, situations, and even people.

Walk onto a used car lot, and your spidey-sense will tingle when the salesman approaches you with a pre-planned pitch. You can recognize a disingenuous brand trying to sell you a product that seems too good to be true. We can smell bullshit a mile away.

That's what you're up against when you try to convince your audience to click, sign up, or trust your brand. It's you versus your audience's gut. You'll need to be persuasive without letting your marketing show when courting a skeptical, lazy, or apathetic audience. Before we can learn to overcome these obstacles, we need to dissect and examine the decision-making process.

GOING WITH YOUR GUT

We like to think that as the most highly evolved species to walk the planet, we navigate life with careful logic untainted by the baggage of emotion. It's a noble idea, but one that diverges from the truth. In reality, we almost never have enough time to rely on complex reasoning to make decisions, so we rely on gut reaction. Recall the decisions you made today, and you'll see that your gut is in the driver's seat.

What shirt should I wear? Hmmm, the blue one looks nice. What should I have for breakfast? I'm hungry for eggs and bacon. Crap, looks like there's traffic ahead. Maybe I'll take this exit to see if I can get around it.

Intuition drives so many decisions we make each day. You're wearing the shirt you have on now because you "just felt like it." You had other appropriate options, but if you used logic to consider each and every one, you'd never make it out the door. The problem is that many times there are several logical options to choose from, and logic can leave us gridlocked, with no clear path to follow. Emotion is the tiebreaking vote when many options are equally valid. You use instinct to choose something that's good enough when the best option is unclear. If it weren't for gut decisions, we'd be lucky to get anything done.

So what would happen if emotion wasn't helping us to make decisions? Antonio Damasio, Professor of Neuroscience at the University of Southern California, has studied people who have injured the areas of the brain responsible for emotion. Basic decisions vex them. Deciding when to schedule a doctor's appointment triggers a circuitous internal debate on the merits of the various options. Similarly, choosing a restaurant for lunch proves impossible, as evaluating pros and cons

Anatomy of a gut decision

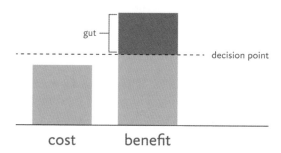

FIG 5.1: To convince skeptics to act, you don't have to make a brilliant case, you just have to offer more benefit than cost so people's gut reaction to your design falls in your favor.

never ends. Where there are many options of similar or equal merit, there's nothing to push these people's thought processes into a final decision. Without the tie-breaking vote the emotional gut response provides, they cannot decide.

As designers, we're in a unique position to help users follow their gut instincts. Using common design tools like layout, color, line, typography, and contrast, we can help people more easily consume information and make a decision driven by instinct more than reason. Just as you chose the shirt you're wearing because it felt right, we can help our audience sign up for a service or complete a task because their gut tells them it's the right thing to do. Remember, we don't have to make an exhaustive case for action because reason is not often the primary driving force our audience uses to decide. We just have to appeal to their emotions to make the benefits appear to outweigh the costs. (FIG 5.1).

If you've ever designed a signup form, you're familiar with the challenge of convincing someone to take action. Subtle changes to button design, language, or layout can sometimes make your conversion rates shoot up or down. But sometimes the secret to better conversion rates is not in the minutiae, but in the big picture. The way type, color, and layout fit together says a lot about a brand and shapes new users' perceptions.

Mint: money is no laughing matter

The hugely popular money management web application, Mint (http://mint.com), had a heck of a challenge when they launched. A service that aggregates your financial information and requires you to share access to all of your bank accounts is bound to attract skeptics. For Mint to succeed, they had to inspire trust.

In theory, investors loved the idea of Mint. A free service that helps people understand how they're spending their money could have real mass appeal, and could make a lot of money by recommending financial products that would help users save money. But venture capitalists had major reservations about Mint because trusting a free service (the word "free" invokes our inner skeptic) to share such personal data was unheard of.

Jason Putorti, Mint's designer, knew that design was going to be central to their success:

> Trust was the most critical barrier for us to overcome with potential users. It was an uphill battle raising venture capital because investors simply didn't think people would ever share bank credentials. Trust is a gut feeling more than a rational process, and visual design affects emotions in a very powerful way, perhaps more than any other stimuli.

Putorti designed Mint to stand out not only from primary competitors like Quicken and TurboTax, but also from other apps on the web. When Mint was founded in 2006, minimalist, function-driven design inspired by apps from 37Signals was the industry standard. With a design agency background, Putorti brought a different aesthetic to the project. Then, web app designers were leery of overusing images to create gradient effects or to render a font that wasn't available to all users. Speed was the primary focus, and texture, illustrations, and typographic exploration were uncommon in web apps. But

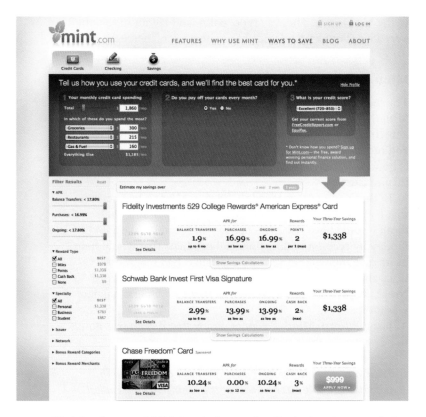

FIG 5.2: Mint's interface uses rich lighting, shadows, and a refined color palette to make it stand out from competitors, while engendering trust in a skeptical audience.

Putorti wasn't carrying these preconceptions when he designed Mint.

In Mint you'll notice a sense of light in the interface that's created by glows, extensive gradients, and shadows. Though data rich, this isn't your dad's Excel spreadsheet. Charts protrude off the page with a bubbly gloss, inviting a lingering gaze. Remember, Gmail and Basecamp were the paragons of web app design in 2006, when Mint was released. Mint stood in stark contrast to the flat designs many web app users were accustomed to seeing (**FIG 5.2**).

The carefully considered interface design and impeccable execution turned skeptics into signups. Mint presented engaging ways to view trends in one's spending habits and offered ways to save money. These are compelling benefits to be sure. If that data were trapped in a poorly designed interface, as is the case with most financial software, the stories of one's financial life would be hard to read, which diminishes the value. Without a strong value proposition, security concerns would almost certainly outweigh the benefits, decreasing the chance of converting skeptics. Design was critical to Mint's success.

The care and consideration apparent in the design gives users the impression that equal attention is paid behind the scenes where Mint manages security and privacy. Sure, Mint makes it clear that your information is securely guarded, but rather than having to constantly reiterate the point in the copy, the design says it more effectively.

You'd trust a bodyguard in a perfectly-pressed black Armani suit more than a guy in cut-off jeans and a ripped Grateful Dead t-shirt, wouldn't you? Appearance can greatly influence perceptions, and we carry that mental model with us when sizing up a website. Mint's sharp design inspires just enough trust to help people value its benefits more than they fear its costs.

Putorti put a lot of stock in the idea that design could be a compelling enough reason to sign up for Mint. Though security was important, he saw it as a secondary challenge:

> Visual aesthetic was key. A financial management app is a different challenge; the information itself has to be presented in a useful way that also delights and excites the user.
>
> Security is not the reason why people sign up for the service. Convenience and information about their money is. If you provide an overwhelming value to the user if they give up a bit of information, most people will do so.

In the end, users' gut reactions were that Mint seemed secure enough and the attractive charts and graphs held enough value that they were willing to take the risk and sign up.

Though investor reservations about Mint were based on solid logic, Mint defied reason by appealing to users' emotions. In November of 2009, Mint was acquired by Quicken—their primary competitor—proving to all that design and emotion are just as valuable as reason and logic, and sometimes maybe even more so.

We can woo skeptics with thoughtful design that serves a strong value proposition, but lazy users require a different line of thinking.

THE PATH OF LEAST RESISTANCE

Skepticism is not the only obstacle we confront when trying to entice our audience to act. Laziness is just as big a hurdle. In truth, people really aren't as lazy as we like to think they are. They're just looking for the path of least resistance to their destination. When people are reluctant to act, sometimes a little incentive gets them moving.

Dropbox: bribery will get you everywhere

Dropbox (http://dropbox.com)—a service that offers synced file storage between computers, mobile devices, and the cloud—has little trouble enticing signups for a free account with 250MB of storage space. Their value proposition makes it easy for new customers to see that Dropbox's benefits out-weigh the cost. Free storage? What's not to like about that? The initial gut reaction to Dropbox is positive.

There is, however, a small catch. To get started with Dropbox you have to install software on at least one com-puter—more if you're syncing between machines—plus you must install the mobile app to access files on your phone. The getting started task sequence is disjointed. Though the indi-vidual workflow steps are relatively straightforward, you must jump from device to device to complete the setup process, so it's easy for Dropbox to lose people along the way. As a new customer invests more time into getting started, the costs can start to seem greater than the benefits.

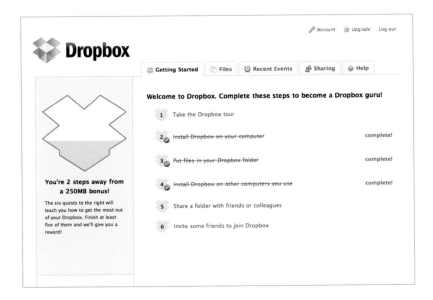

FIG 5.3: Dropbox helps new users become invested in their system with a game that rewards those who complete it with free additional storage space.

Dropbox is also not your typical software as a service. It's a web app, but it's also a desktop and mobile app at the same time. That's new territory for a lot of people, and there's a learning curve to using the service as well as understanding how it will make your life easier. Getting people in the door is easy for Dropbox. It's retaining users and getting them invested that's tricky.

Dropbox has a novel approach to getting their audience invested immediately on sign up. They've created a game with a handsome reward awaiting those who complete it. When a new customer logs into Dropbox, they're presented with six simple tasks (**FIG 5.3**).

To win more storage space, users must take a tour, install Dropbox on their computer, put files in their Dropbox folder, install the software on other machines, share folders with friends, and then tell others about the service. A meter indicating task completion and progress toward the 250MB storage

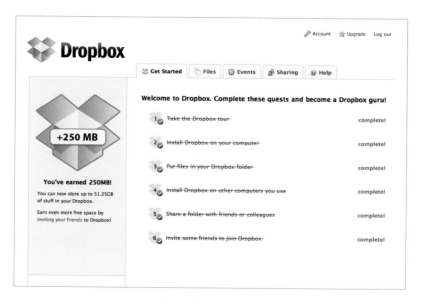

FIG 5.4: The meter on the left fills to display the Dropbox logo upon completion of the tasks.

space reward accompanies the tasks. It feels like a game to the user, but Dropbox is decreasing the chance of account abandonment by educating people on how to use the system, and its value to their digital life. Once your files are in Dropbox, and you've shared them with friends, the cost of canceling is higher than continuing to use the service.

Call it bribery, call it game theory. The result is the same. Users feel a sense of accomplishment when they've completed the required tasks (**FIG 5.4**), and with more free space, they're excited to drop more stuff into Dropbox. The game of earning free space continues when users post to Twitter and Facebook about the service to encourage others to sign up. As we'll see in the final chapter, game theory, bribery, and achievement works on brochureware websites, too.

Dealing with skeptics is difficult, but at least they're paying attention to your message. What do you do if your audience just isn't that into you?

APATHY

Skepticism and laziness are troubling obstacles to confront, but apathy is worse. It's demoralizing to launch a website or app that you've spent countless hours designing and building, only to see your hard work adrift on a sea of indifference.

Users react apathetically to websites when the content is irrelevant to their interests, or when content is poorly presented. Content strategy will help you create the right content for your audience. It's beyond our present scope, but read Erin Kissane's book *The Elements of Content Strategy* if content creation is a stumbling point for you (http://bkaprt.com/cs).

In the examples we've seen so far in this book, great content was always at the core. Intelligent delivery methods complemented the content by either providing new, engaging pathways into the content, or by retaining audience interest. Great content delivered in an emotionally engaging manner is like kryptonite for apathy.

Let's return to examples from previous chapters. Do you remember Betabrand from Chapter 1? It's an ecommerce site that sells men's clothing, which is a competitive market sector. Betabrand keeps their audience interested through well-crafted content. They have nearly thirty minutes of hilarious content for each product line. Their customers buy because the content makes them feel good, and they return because the site experience is memorable. Betabrand's audience is anything but apathetic.

In the Housing Works example from Chapter 3, content was at the heart of their emotional design strategy. First-person stories and client portraits help the audience to create an emotional connection to the organization. Human stories are what draw their audience into the website, and get people involved in their cause.

Don't despair if your audience is less than enthusiastic about your site. In the next section I'll help you get things back on track.

IF AT FIRST YOU DON'T SUCCEED...

If after implementing this book's ideas and recommendations your audience is still apathetic toward your site, ask yourself these questions:

- Is the personality I've created for my brand authentic and well matched to the profile of my audience?
- Is my brand personality too similar to those of my competitors?
- Is my content well written and relevant to my audience's needs and interests?
- Do the emotional design methods I'm using interfere with the base layers of the user's hierarchy of needs (making the site less functional, reliable, usable)?

You may have a hard time answering these questions honestly, in which case you might conduct simple user research and usability tests to evaluate your assumptions. Do you have access to people in your target audience? Round up three to six people to meet in person or via Skype (http://skype.com) or GoToMeeting (http://gotomeeting.com). Ask your users open-ended questions that will give you the insights you seek. You might ask things like:

- Describe your initial reactions to the website.
- How does the website make you feel?
- If this website were a person, who would it be and why?
- Would you recommend this site to a friend? Why or why not?
- Are there site sections or features that are more important to you than others? Less important? Why?

Avoid asking questions that bait the user into answering in a particular way. For instance, a question like "Do you think this website has a pleasant personality?" skews answers toward the affirmative, because the question's language primes the user's perceptions. Remember those priming techniques discussed in the previous chapter? You want to avoid them here so you can collect honest and accurate insights about your website.

Conduct simple usability tests with three users by following Steve Krug's methods from his best-selling book *Don't Make Me Think.* The results will help you better understand whether or not your emotional design strategies are impeding your site's usability, reliability, or functionality. Krug recommends rounding up site users, buying some nice snacks, inviting the head honchos of your organization, and conducting very simple usability tests that direct users through workflows that you want to evaluate. Record the sessions with software like Silverback (http://silverbackapp.com), and review the videos to evaluate the user's facial expression at key points in the interface. Did they smile at that point of surprise and delight or did they simply ignore it and move on?

Keep these tests simple and practical to ensure you actually do them and get the insights that will help you improve your website. Though less scientific than targeting people in your audience, you could simply visit your local coffee shop and offer a latté and a muffin to a few patrons for ten minutes of their time. When it comes down to it, any testing is better than no testing.

Disinterest in your site can be vexing, but most of the time you can understand that disinterest by talking to your audience. Sure, finding time to talk to real people in your audience can be tough. But when you're hitting a wall of apathy, it can be the best way to correct your course and move forward.

MEA CULPA

Emotional design is not just about creating positive experiences and overcoming obstacles. It can also help us deal with difficult situations like server downtime, lost data, or bugs that affect a user's workflow. Mistakes happen. Things go wrong. But a well-crafted response, and the cache of trust you accrue with your audience through prolonged emotional engagement, can save you in times of trouble, as we'll see in the coming chapter.

6 FORGIVENESS

SOONER OR LATER, something will go wrong with your website. Servers go down, people make mistakes, and the unforeseeable happens. In such situations, it's helpful to have your audience's goodwill on your side so they will more easily overlook a temporary shortcoming and maintain trust in your brand.

As we've seen in previous chapters, your audience performs an internal cost/benefit analysis every time you ask them to complete a task. The results of this internal assessment determine whether or not a user acts. When something goes awry and your audience is inconvenienced, there is a risk that users will suddenly perceive the costs of using your site as greater than the benefits. Emotional engagement before and even during a major event can help mitigate the risk of losing your audience.

In fact, when you create a compelling experience, your audience will often forget about the inconveniences they've encountered over time and just remember the good things about your brand. So long as the good outweighs the bad, you win. That's why you must accrue goodwill as an insurance policy for the problems that are certain to occur.

Flickr knows from first-hand experience that a good response to a bad situation is critical. It doesn't hurt to have a fanatical fan base too, as we'll see.

FLICKR: TURNING LEMONS INTO LEMONADE

In July 2006, a storage failure struck Flickr, the popular photo sharing service. Though photos were safe and no data was lost, thousands of enthusiastic users were inconvenienced as their favorite photo site took a temporary nap (roughly three hours). Tensions ran high as engineers worked to bring the site back online. Inquiries from concerned users poured in.

During the crisis, the Flickr team had a stroke of genius. Thinking like a veteran parent trying to keep an antsy kid occupied while waiting for food in a restaurant, they applied the art of redirection and ran a coloring contest. They posted a message that explained the outage, asked users to print the page, and do something creative with it to win a free, one-year Flickr Pro account (**FIG 6.1**).

Rather than brooding over their missing photo library, users brainstormed ways to win the prize. Hundreds of entries were submitted—some of which were very clever (**FIG 6.2**).

Though the site was down and many were inconvenienced, Flickr users remember the fun they had participating in the coloring contest, and for some, how great it was to win a free year of Pro service.

All's well that ends well, but there are lessons we can learn from Flickr's experience as we confront our own errors and struggle to suppress customer mutiny. Confronting the negative emotions that arise in situations like this is important, and the experience you've designed around your site just might save you.

Flickr worked through the stressful situation by communicating calmly and honestly with their users. Let's take a closer look at how Flickr handled the event to learn how emotional design shaped user reactions.

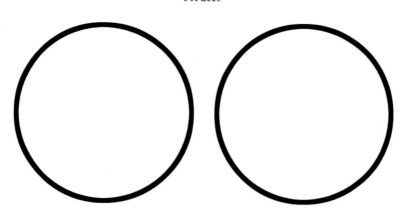

Arrggh! Our tubes are clogged!

Because this sucks*, we thought you might like to enter an impromptu competition to win a FREE PRO ACCOUNT!

Just print out this page and colour in the dots. When the site's back up, take a photo of your creation and post it to Flickr, tagged with "flickrcolourcontest".

Team Flickr will pick a winner in the next couple of days, and that lucky duck will get a free year of Pro.

* Seriously, we apologise for the unannounced downtime. We're working as fast as we can to get flickr.com back online. **Details here**.

FIG 6.1: During a major outage in July of 2006, Flickr ran a coloring contest that turned stressed users into content contestants.

Responding to events: facts before fun

During events like the one Flickr experienced, the right tone is essential to ease concerns. When people are deeply stressed by an outage or a mistake you've made, you must explain what happened swiftly, honestly, and clearly. Give people the facts of the event, communicate that you're doing your best to resolve things, then update users regularly, even if not much has changed. That's exactly what Flickr did via their blog as the event unfolded (http://bkaprt.com/de/8).

FIG 6.2: People went nuts over the Flickr coloring contest, submitting clever entries that won a select few a free Pro account. Photos by KC Soon (http://bkaprt.com/de/9, left) and Bart Kung (http://bkaprt.com/de/10, right).

Updates let people know you're still focusing all of your attention on resolving the problem. They give you another opportunity to apologize for the inconvenience and reassure your users that you'll fix the problem as quickly as possible.

Once you've done your best to soften emotions, you might consider a redirection like Flickr's. Giving users something for free can rekindle the good will you've worked so hard to cultivate and gives them something else to focus on while you do your best to fix the problem. If giving something to everyone isn't possible, a contest is a nice way to achieve the same redirection effect while limiting the expenses you may incur.

In high-stress situations, your top priority must be to tame negative emotions as best you can and, if possible, shift them back to the positive.

Although their clever response to the outage helped save the day for Flickr, it wasn't the only reason their users stuck with them in a time of crisis.

The unsung hero in Flickr's outage recovery

What really saved Flickr on July 19, 2006, was not just a clever coloring contest, it was the emotional design in their website that has accrued user devotion. Flickr is an icon in emotional design, creating an informal and human personality within the interface that makes it a joy to use. We all love the multilingual greetings we see upon signing in and it's always a hoot when cuddly panda bears appear in the interface. The coloring contest was simply another way for the design persona that has earned them a devoted following to manifest itself. Sure, people get upset when they can't access one of their favorite web apps, but a long history of great experiences with the site trumps the inconvenience of an outage.

Emotional design is your insurance to maintain audience trust when things aren't going your way. If you've ever been emotionally committed to someone who has hurt you, you know that the human response to such situations is driven by gut feeling more than by logic. You don't add up the good and bad experiences in your mind and do a detailed comparison before deciding whether or not to maintain ties with the person. You simply respond based on the strength of your emotional commitment. We react similarly to products and services.

Emotional engagement can help us look past even the most serious infractions, leaving the good more prominent in our mind than the bad. Psychologists call this phenomenon of positive recollection the rosy effect. As time passes, memories of inconveniences and transgressions fade, leaving only positive memories to shape our perceptions.

This is good news for designers, as it means that the inevitable imperfections in our work don't necessarily lead to mass user exodus. In his article entitled "Memory is more important than actuality" (http://bkaprt.com/de/11), Donald Norman points out that pursuing perfection is a spurious goal, as the total experience we're creating will shape our users' memories of our work in the end.

As interaction designers, we strive to eliminate confusion, difficulty, and above all, bad experiences. But you know what? Life is filled with bad experiences. Not only do we survive them, but in our remembrance of events, we often minimize the bad and amplify the good.

We should not be devoting all of our time to provide a perfect experience. Why not? Well, perfection is seldom possible. More importantly, perfection is seldom worth the effort. So what if people have some problems with an application, a website, a product, or a service? What matters is the total experience. Furthermore, the actual experience is not as important as the way it is remembered.

Though carefully and considerately responding to site mistakes and problems will help get you out of hot water, the emotional design groundwork you lay before an event will keep your audience committed to your brand. The forgiveness we earn through careful emotional design can prevent considerable losses in customers and revenues, which is alone a compelling enough reason to incorporate it into our design process.

In the next and final chapter, we'll confront the risks we run when we design for emotion, and see concrete evidence that the rewards make very good business sense.

RISK & REWARD

SHOWING EMOTION IN DESIGN, as in life, is risky. Some people won't get it. Some people will even hate it. But that's okay. An emotional response to your design is far better than indifference.

Emotional design does more than entice and keep your audience, it helps ensure you're talking to the right people. Not every customer is right for your business. Some will be so high maintenance that they will cost you more than they contribute. That can be a real morale and financial drag.

If people complain about how your product, service, or brand are unlike your competitors', then you're doing something right (so long as they're not complaining about service quality, reliability, etc.). The people who don't understand you will come around as the passion for your brand increases. Certain people just need others' validation before they can fall in love with a product or service. Though our instincts might tell us that it's risky being different, the greater risk is in being the same as your competitors, as you make it harder for people to understand why your brand is the better choice.

We've looked at many techniques and examples in this book, but nothing communicates emotional design's value better than hard data. As we wrap up, I'd like to leave you with some empirical evidence that can help you influence your boss and colleagues into taking a calculated risk with emotional design.

PUTTING IT INTO PRACTICE

I hope that you're fired up about designing stuff that will have a lasting influence on your audience. But, it may be difficult to channel your passions into your work if your boss doesn't see the value in designing for emotion. When your boss or client says, "I don't know. This emotional design stuff sounds risky," you need to be ready with case studies and an action plan that will make even the staunchest skeptic see that your ideas are good for the bottom line. Before we hatch a plan that will win over the folks in charge, let's look at three real-world examples with hard data to bolster your arguments and silence your critics.

Starting small: CoffeeCup Software

To design for emotion, you don't have to redesign your site or rebrand. It's okay, and even advisable, to start small. Try simple experiments in a section of your site and limit them to a short time period. That's exactly what CoffeeCup Software (http://coffeecup.com) did in the spring of 2010.

With Easter approaching, CoffeeCup created a fun easter egg hunt on their site. Their goals were very simple. They wanted to attract more traffic and increase sales. Their expectations were very business focused, but modest.

Their team scurried about the site like little bunnies cleverly hiding easter eggs that would only be displayed at certain times of the day, or only after a set number of page views (**FIG 7.1**). This was no kindergarten egg hunt; it took some real searching to find a winning egg. Those that did find one were rewarded with free software packs or cash.

We've hidden over $18,000 worth of cash and software all over our site. All you have to do is find it.

FIG 7.1: CoffeeCup Software ran an easter egg hunt on their site, and saw some amazing results.

J. Cornelius, CoffeeCup's VP of Operations, kicked off the hunt with a quick tweet (FIG 7.2).

Shortly thereafter, word spread on Twitter and Facebook, and site traffic began to swell. In the first three days, traffic tripled. Before the egg hunt, CoffeeCup would typically get about five page views per visitor, but once the egg hunt began, they saw an average of 30 page views per visitor. People spent hours and hours on the site in search of a winning egg. One user confessed on the Facebook fan page that she spent five hours searching for a winning egg, and in the end, it turned her into a customer:

> So pleased to have found this software. I've wanted it for a while and was saving up. Now I can treat myself to some of the other software I have been studying and trying during my 5 hour egg hunt.

Check out what forum user "paintbrush" had to say about her reaction to the contest (http://bkaprt.com/de/12):

> Just can't let it go. Into 3rd day now. Ashamed of how many hours I've spent. By the way, I've clicked on every egg I saw - right from the beginning (started at 10:15 Mon.) - all taken!

@CoffeeCup
CoffeeCup Software

We've hidden over $20,000 in cash and software on our Website! Just find an egg and claim what's inside.
http://bit.ly/ccegg

29 Mar 10 via Echofon   ☆ Favorite   ⟲ Retweet   ↰ Reply

Retweeted by globalundo and 4 others

FIG 7.2: The CoffeeCup easter egg hunt was kicked off by a tweet from the VP of Operations, J. Cornelius.

When could any of us say we had a single visitor spend three days on our site? CoffeeCup's forums exploded with chatter about the promotion. More than 3,700 posts were made, which received more than 55,000 views.

The egg hunt had a lasting effect on CoffeeCup's social networking reach. They had a 217% increase in Facebook fans and a 170% increase in Twitter followers. Because of their experiment, they've been able to stay in touch with more customers.

CoffeeCup's promotion statistics are staggering. They used many of the design principles we saw in earlier chapters, including variable rewards, anticipation, the velvet rope effect, and status, creating a very powerful effect. Though the numbers are kept private, they did indeed see a sales spike.

CoffeeCup ran the experiment for a limited time, after which the site returned to its old self, and the risks of the emotional design principles they used faded. However, we can agree that the risk they faced didn't compare to what they gained.

The same holds true for Blue Sky Resumes, a company that took a chance on emotional design, and won big.

Going big: Blue Sky Resumes' redesign

If you're starting a new site, and you have the stones to go further, you can weave brand, design, and message together into a broader emotional design strategy. Blue Sky Resumes (http://blueskyresumes.com/), a service that helps people craft a great resume, did just that in their 2010 website redesign. Squared Eye, (http://squaredeye.com), a North Carolina-based design agency headed by Matthew Smith, led the redesign.

Before starting, Squared Eye looked at the websites of Blue Sky Resumes' competitors. Many had a similar look, with cheesy stock photography, stodgy type and colors, and an overall generic feel. They all had a milquetoast personality, which doesn't exactly inspire confidence in a company that could play a central role in your career.

After Able Design (http://designedbyable.com) rebranded Blue Sky, Squared Eye designed a website showing Blue Sky Resumes as a clear choice for young, tech-savvy professionals who don't want to be just another applicant in a pile of resumes. By narrowing down the audience, Squared Eye enjoyed creative latitude to design a brand personality, avoiding the generic, design-for-everyone approach that so many other résumé services cling to.

Playing off the company name, the site design (**FIG 7.3**) conveys a hopeful future, which is a powerful message especially since the global recession had left many unemployed.

The header's gently floating clouds, witty copy, and the strong but informal slab serif heading font are a few site design elements that let visitors know that like them, Blue Sky Resumes is unique. Matthew Smith describes his process:

I wanted to incorporate not only a fresh fun design, but also techniques that would be used and loved by the modern web, and so we introduced the use of @font-face, and an uncommon

FIG 7.3: When Blue Sky Resumes site redesign created an informal and fun personality, it dramatically improved conversions.

layout system to enhance the design personality. All of these techniques combined with strong photography and clever moments of fun made for a site that felt enjoyable and energetic. We tested our hypothesis against some of Blue Sky Resumes' clientele and it was getting rave reviews.

When Blue Sky launched their new website, they felt confident it would help their business, but didn't anticipate the results they saw. The new website increased the number of monthly proposal requests by 15%. The average revenue earned from each client grew by 15%. They saw a 65% increase in clients each month, and a staggering 85% increase in total revenues. Their conversion rate climbed from an already good 25% to 36%.

In short, with their new website, Blue Sky Resumes boosted business by reaching the right people with which to forge lasting relationships. Here's what's really impressive about these stats: Blue Sky Resumes changed *nothing else* about their marketing. Their improved conversion rates and increased revenues are all because of a redesign that made emotional design a priority.

Louise Fletcher, co-founder of Blue Sky Resumes, has some interesting insight into why their numbers shot up so impressively after the redesign.

> *These numbers show that the biggest impact the site design made has been to pre-convert prospects into clients—in other words, they are already convinced before they contact us. Hence the almost 50% boost in our conversion rate.*

Shortly after the redesign, *Oprah Magazine*'s Creative Director contacted Blue Sky Resumes asking to feature them in an article about performing a career makeover for some deserving women. Why did *Oprah Magazine* pick Blue Sky? Because their website presented them as a human company that has its customers' best interests at heart. They don't come across like their competitors who churn through as many résumés as possible to make a buck. Blue Sky Resumes appreciates the individual, and their site design shows it.

There were times when Blue Sky was a little nervous about Squared Eye's design direction. It felt risky because it was so different from what they were used to. But in the end, expressing the personality of the business is what boosted Blue Sky Resumes' business.

Blue Sky Resumes went all in with their redesign and CoffeeCup took a measured, temporary approach. There is a third option that sits somewhere in between.

Middle ground: progressively enhance

You can experiment with emotional design with small, temporary changes like we saw with CoffeeCup Software, or you can go all the way in a rebrand and redesign as Blue Sky Resumes did. There's another alternative you can explore when designing for emotion. If you read *A List Apart,* a magazine for people who make websites, you already know about progressive enhancement (http://bkaprt.com/de/13), a concept that encourages building websites to serve the needs of many, while layering enhancements atop a solid foundation to offer a rich experience for those with a more capable browser.

Progressive enhancement is second nature to those of us who build standards-based websites. It's a concept that translates to user experience design as well.

In Chapter 4, I shared some insight about the emotional design techniques we've employed in MailChimp's interface. The humor and fun we've laced into the experience has built us a loyal following, but there's another side to that story. Though most people get a kick out of it, some people flat out hate the jokes in the app. It's just not their style. Just as similar personalities can unite to create symbiotic bliss, other personalities are incompatible like oil and water.

Though we weren't willing to forfeit our brand personality because some people don't identify with it, we found a solution that quieted the occasional tweet or support ticket complaining about the design persona. We created an option in the app settings that allows users to disable the fun stuff by turning on "party pooper mode." It turns off all greetings and buttons up the informal language peppered throughout the interface, making it straight-laced enough for those afraid their clients won't get the jokes and for people who are just fuddy duddies.

I'll be honest with you: on principle, I was opposed to creating party pooper mode to appease occasional complaints. It felt like we were giving up the thing that made us most unique to be everything to everyone. Though my reservations came from the right place, my concerns about how it would change our brand were wrong.

After party pooper mode had been out for over a year, we wondered how many of our users actually turned it on. I was half scared to find out, because if it were a majority, it would be a referendum on the design persona we had painstakingly constructed. As it turns out, only 0.007% of users actually turn on party pooper mode. What we learned is that even though there are a few vocal party poopers who don't get the MailChimp brand, there are far more people who *do* get it and love the moments of joy the application brings. In my opinion, that's well worth a little risk.

Progressive enhancement may be a worthwhile option in your design as well. It can mitigate client or boss concerns, quieting those who don't understand your personality.

The numbers are in. We've seen hard evidence of emotional design's value, but there's just one problem left to solve. How do you convince your boss to give it a shot?

CONVINCING YOUR BOSS

Convincing your boss or client to sign off on site changes that may have a big effect on the organization can be tough, and maybe even a little scary. Now that you have some detailed case studies with compelling data to bolster your arguments, all you need is a plan.

Let's start with the big picture. Is your organization or client willing and able to rebrand or redesign the website to build a better connection to your audience? If a total redesign is out, would smaller changes to refine the brand or site design be viable? If you answered yes to either of these questions, start with a design persona as discussed in Chapter 3.

Even if your brand is already connecting with your audience, a design persona can be a good exercise to focus you on the relationship you want to build with your audience and the relationship they want to build with you. It's a nice tool to have as you kick off discussions with your boss about your ideas for emotional design. Instead of making a case by saying, "I think it would be great if we...," you can reference your design persona document and say, "Our brand personality is this..., and by doing this...we'll stand out from competitors while building a much better connection with our customers." Connect your ideas to business goals and avoid opinion-based arguments. You'll make a strong case that will be harder to dismiss.

Science and psychology have figured prominently in the examples we've seen in this book. As you pitch your ideas to those in charge, don't be afraid to reference the principles you've learned. We know that emotional design isn't about nice-to-have warm fuzzy experiences: it's central to daily life and the decision-making process for consumers. The more effectively you can employ emotional design in your site, the better conversion rates and sales will be.

Use the case studies in this book as a starting point for the conversation. Showing your boss that you've been doing independent research about how to improve the site you work on demonstrates admirable chutzpah, starting the conversation with an immediate win in your column. Raise please! Tie a case study or two to some stuff you've been working on and the head honcho will see the relevance to your organization. Make sure your examples are brand-appropriate for your organization so your boss stays focused on your concepts and doesn't get lost in the details of implementation. Remember, emotional design should never interfere with usability, functionality, or reliability.

Rather than trying to revolutionize everything on the site at once, pick one key metric you'd like to improve, such as average time on the site, or the number of sales inquiries. Tweak the interface using principles of emotional design, then use something like Google Site Optimizer (http://bkaprt.com/de/14) to test the changes against the original design. If your target metric improves, you have a rock solid case to present to your boss for implementing emotional design in other places in the site. You can't argue with numbers.

When you're the person in charge, change almost always smells of risk. Your job is to communicate the great gains your organization can achieve, and show that small risks are well worth it.

CONCLUSION

We've come a long way in this little volume, through design and psychology principles applied by Wufoo, Betabrand, Housing Works, Mint, Flickr, and Blue Sky Resumes, to name a few. Despite the vast differences in audience, content, and design, there is a common thread to them all. Each site we've seen values craft and a strong sense of personality that lets their users see the humans at the other end of the connection.

Carefully considered content and well-executed design work in concert in these websites. Though functional, reliable, and usable, the sites we've seen go a step further to create a pleasurable experience. Emotional design connects with an audience in ways we could have never fathomed when we were designing websites that inflated our public persona with an insincere facade that nobody gave a damn about. Today, we can channel our own personality into our work so our users can feel like they're interacting with a real human—not a corporate avatar. They love us for our sincerity, they trust us because they see themselves in our brand, and when we make inevitable mistakes, they'll be more likely to forgive us because our earnestness is visible.

In Chapter 3, I asked you to recall an encounter with a person that made a strong impression on you when you first met. You had so much in common that it was easy to share a joke or a personal story. You left feeling that you'd just made a real human connection. Do you still have that memory? I hope so, because that's your standard as you begin to design for emotion.

We're not just designing pages. We're designing human experiences. Like the visionaries of the Arts and Crafts movement, we know that preserving the human touch and showing ourselves in our work isn't optional: *it's essential.*

ACKNOWLEDGEMENTS

This book would not be resting in your hands if not for the generous opportunity afforded me by Jeffrey Zeldman, Mandy Brown, and Jason Santa Maria. I'm honored to be the purple stripe in A Book Apart's "rainbow of knowledge" and humbled to be part of such a brilliant line up of authors.

I owe a great deal of thanks to Mandy Brown and Krista Stevens, who made me look like a better writer than I am. They were patient with me when I bumbled through certain passages, and kindly offered a pat on the back just when I needed it. Mandy and Krista, you made writing this book fun, and for that I thank you.

Whitney Hess shared invaluable feedback on early drafts that kept me pointed in the right direction. I'm grateful to have had her expert opinion and eagle eye on this book.

I've long admired Jared Spool for his intelligent user experience research, and his willingness to help us all better serve the needs of our users. What a treat and a privilege it is for me to have him introduce readers to this book.

I spent a lot of time researching for this book, but I had some indispensable help from Ben Chestnut and Matthew Smith. Ben fed me a steady stream of inspiration and examples for more than a year. He's also created a one-of-a-kind work place in which I've been able to experiment with the ideas I've just shared with you. For that, I am eternally grateful.

After a quick email asking him to keep his eyes pealed for examples of emotional design, Matthew Smith generously sent me countless examples that kept my wheels turning. Thanks, Matthew.

Tyrick Christian so kindly helped me refine the presentation of the design persona examples from Chapter 3. He helped me realize my vision for them, while making them flexible for all to use. I'm lucky to have had his help.

Writing a book is hard work, and it helps to have a support system to keep your spirits high. My wife Jamie generously shouldered baby duties to free me up to write, and showered me with encouragement when I needed it most. She fuels my fire like no other. How fortunate am I to make time with her.

I became a father shortly before I started writing this book. My son Olivier has taught me even more about emotional design than the brilliant designers and thinkers I've cited here. I'm a better person for his tutelage, and for that I thank him.

RESOURCES

Design principles are an essential guide as we solve visual and conceptual problems. Let's face it, if you don't have a solid foundation in basic design principles you're destined to succumb to the temptations of decoration and design without meaning. If you can buy but one design book, make it *Universal Principles of Design* (http://bkaprt.com/de/15).

Speaking of design principles, designer, author, and speaker Stephen Anderson has spent a great deal of time researching the principles of emotional design. He's kindly shared his insights in the form of a handy deck of cards called Mental Notes (http://bkaprt.com/de/16). Each card presents a new principle of emotional design.

I'm certainly not the first person to see the connection between design and emotion. The legendary design thinker, Donald Norman, searches for the reasons we fall in love with products in his timeless book *Emotional Design* (http://bkaprt.com/de/17).

There's a lot of science and psychology behind the concepts and techniques we explored in this book. If you want to dig deeper still into the fascinating magic happening between our ears, start with Stephen Pinker's *How the Mind Works* (http://bkaprt.com/de/18), and Antonio Domasio's *Descartes' Error* (http://bkaprt.com/de/19).

Youngme Moon's book *Different* (http://bkaprt.com/de/20) takes a look at why some brands manage to stand out and become meaningfully different.

Dr. John Medina provides a great deal of insight into the relationships between the way our brains are structured and the way we behave. You'll find his book *Brain Rules* an interesting read (http://bkaprt.com/de/21).

If you're just getting started or still getting your bearings with user experience design, you're certain to find *A Project Guide to UX Design* a useful reference (http://bkaprt.com/de/22).

You'll find a host of compelling articles exploring psychology, emotion, and user experience design at UXMag. Here are a few of my favorites:

- Dana Chisnell, "Beyond Frustration" (http://bkaprt.com/de/23)
- Susan Weinschenk, "The Psychologist's View of UX Design" (http://bkaprt.com/de/24)
- Nathanael Boehm, "Organized Approach to Emotional Response Testing" (http://bkaprt.com/de/25)

Trevor van Gorp looks at the role of personality in emotional design in his article "Emotional Design with A.C.T.: Part 1" (http://bkaprt.com/de/26).

The full transcripts from the interviews I conducted with designers for this book, and a host of other resources for the emotional design enthusiast, await you on my blog, where I continue to share my research: http://aarronwalter.com/tag/emotional-design

REFERENCES

Shortened URLs are numbered sequentially; the related long URLs are listed below for reference.

Chapter 1

1 http://twitter.com/rainnwilson/status/20347529530
2 http://gettingreal.37signals.com/

Chapter 3

3 http://www.flickr.com/photos/clagnut/4947389773
4 http://en.wikipedia.org/wiki/File:Bundesarchiv_Bild_146II-732,_Erholung_am_Flussufer.jpg
5 http://www.webdesignerdepot.com/2008/12/why-mood-boards-matter/
6 http://daringfireball.net/linked/2009/04/02/designing-convertbot

Chapter 4

7 http://dribbble.com/shots/14379-Profile

Chapter 6

8 http://blog.flickr.net/en/2006/07/19/temporary-storage-glitch/
9 http://www.flickr.com/photos/14922438@N00/194463892/
10 http://www.flickr.com/photos/41225983@N00/193706751/
11 http://interactions.acm.org/content/?p=1226

Chapter 7

12 http://www.coffeecup.com/forums/search/?q=%22Guess+I+could+have+waited+for+today+if+all%22&in=81&type=contents&view=posts&search=true&button_search.x=54&button_search.y=-106&button_search=true
13 http://www.alistapart.com/articles/understandingprogressiveenhancement/
14 http://google.com/websiteoptimizer

Resources

15 http://amzn.com/1592535879

16 http://getmentalnotes.com/

17 http://amzn.com/0465051367

18 http://amzn.com/0393334775

19 http://amzn.com/014303622X

20 http://amzn.com/030746086X

21 http://amzn.com/0979777747

22 http://amzn.com/0321607376

23 http://uxmag.com/design/beyond-frustration-three-levels-of-happy-design

24 http://uxmag.com/design/the-psychologists-view-of-ux-design

25 http://uxmag.com/design/organized-approach-to-emotional-response-testing

26 http://boxesandarrows.com/view/emotional-design

INDEX

ABOUT A BOOK APART

Web design is about multi-disciplinary mastery and laser focus, and that's the thinking behind our brief books for people who make websites. We cover the emerging and essential topics in web design and development with style, clarity, and, above all, brevity—because working designer-developers can't afford to waste time.

The goal of every title in our catalog is to shed clear light on a tricky subject, and do it fast, so you can get back to work. Thank you for supporting our mission to provide professionals with the tools they need to move the web forward.

COLOPHON

The text is set in FF Yoga and its companion, FF Yoga Sans, both by Xavier Dupré. Headlines and cover are set in Titling Gothic by David Berlow.

ABOUT THE AUTHOR

Aarron Walter (http://aarronwalter.com) is the lead user experience designer for MailChimp, where he socializes with primates and ponders ways to make interfaces more human. In a past life, Aarron spent ten glorious years teaching budding web designers at colleges around the US. Today, he channels his passion for education through The Web Standards Project's InterACT curriculum (http://interact. webstandards.org). Aarron lives with his wife and son in Athens, Georgia, and is a wannabe barista.

Photo by Josh Rosenbaum